Asia and the Subprime Crisis

Also by Chi Lo

UNDERSTANDING CHINA'S GROWTH: Forces that Drive China's Economic Future

PHANTOM OF THE CHINA ECONOMIC THREAT: Shadow of the Next Asian Crisis

THE MISUNDERSTOOD CHINA: Uncovering the Truth Behind the Bamboo Curtain

WHEN ASIA MEETS CHINA IN THE NEW MILLENNIUM: China's Role in Shaping Asia's Post-Crisis Economic Transformation

Asia and the Subprime Crisis

Lifting the Veil on the 'Financial Tsunami'

Chi Lo
Economic Strategist, Hong Kong

First published 2009 by
PALGRAVE MACMILLAN

Palgrave Macmillan in the UK is an imprint of Macmillan Publishers Limited, registered in England, company number 785998, of Houndmills, Basingstoke, Hampshire RG21 6XS.

Palgrave Macmillan in the US is a division of St Martin's Press LLC, 175 Fifth Avenue, New York, NY 10010.

Palgrave Macmillan is the global academic imprint of the above companies and has companies and representatives throughout the world.

Palgrave® and Macmillan® are registered trademarks in the United States, the United Kingdom, Europe and other countries.

ISBN: 978–0–230–23619–6 hardback

This book is printed on paper suitable for recycling and made from fully managed and sustained forest sources. Logging, pulping and manufacturing processes are expected to conform to the environmental regulations of the country of origin.

A catalogue record for this book is available from the British Library.

A catalog record for this book is available from the Library of Congress.

10 9 8 7 6 5 4 3 2 1
18 17 16 15 14 13 12 11 10 09

Printed and bound in Great Britain by
CPI Antony Rowe, Chippenham and Eastbourne

For my parents, Margaret, BunBun and ChungChung

Live in happiness
Inquire with openness
Love with passion
Youth becomes eternal

Contents

List of Tables and Charts   viii

Acknowledgements   x

Preface   xi

Introduction   1

1 The Basics of the 'Financial Tsunami'   7

2 The Asian Relevance to the Subprime Crisis   15

3 The Subprime Impact on China   25

4 Macroeconomic Implications and China   39

5 Regulatory Lessons from the Rescue Efforts   49

6 What Can We Learn from AIG's Collapse?   61

7 Different Lessons from Lehman Brothers and Fortis   70

8 Quantitative Easing: a Subprime Antidote?   79

9 Life After Subprime   91

10 China After Subprime   109

Bibliography   123

Index   125

Tables and Charts

Tables

3.1   Chinese banks' exposure to the US
      subprime crisis   26
3.2   Urban fixed-asset investment breakdown   34

Charts

1.1   Anatomy of the subprime crisis   8
1.2   US prime lending rate   9
1.3   US current account deficit   13
2.1   Current account balances before crisis   16
2.2   Loan-to-deposit ratios before crisis   17
2.3   Foreign debt before crisis   17
2.4   US bank loan growth   19
3.1   Chinese banks holding fewer foreign assets   27
3.2   Improving Chinese bank asset quality   28
3.3   Loan-to-deposit ratios   28
3.4   Three-month China interbank offered rate   29
3.5   Net exports' contribution to nominal GDP growth   30
3.6   RMB real effective exchange rate   30
3.7   China's export growth   31
3.8   Chinese exports to the USA, Europe and Japan   32
3.9   Exports absorbing capacity utilisation   33
3.10 Chinese corporate liability/asset ratio   36
3.11 Falling loan-to-deposit ratio   37
4.1   Lopsided growth   40
4.2   China's falling consumption   43
4.3   Exports driving investment   44
4.4   Prolonged decline in real interest rate   45
4.5   Consumer loans remain minimal in China   47
5.1   Loan-to-deposit ratios   54
6.1   Rescuing AIG   64
6.2   Collusion to manipulate CDS price   68

8.1	The Fed in QE drive	80
8.2	US financial institutions tightening lending standards	81
8.3	US money multiplier has collapsed	82
8.4	Declining money velocity	83
8.5	Euro zone money multiplier has also collapsed	84
8.6	Japan's money multiplier collapsed	86
8.7	Japan bank loan growth	86
8.8	Falling inflationary pressures after Japan's asset bubble burst	88
8.9	Chinese urban residents' future inflation expectations	89
8.10	China's inherent deflation problem	90
9.1	Asia has not learned its lessons	93
9.2	Rising Indian GDP growth...	94
9.3	...boosted by capital inflows	95
9.4	Credit growth outpacing GDP growth	96
9.5	India's current account balance	96
9.6	India has the worst fiscal balance	97
9.7	Asian foreign debt	97
9.8	Exports absorbing China's capacity utilisation	100
9.9	Exports driving Chinese investment	100
9.10	World official gold holdings	107
10.1	Chinese consumption falling steadily	111
10.2	Household medical and medicine expenses	112
10.3	Consumer goods/100 households	113
10.4	Initial signs of structural shift in growth	115
10.5	Growth rebalancing	115
10.6	Investment reshuffling towards inland	116
10.7	Big government is returning	119
10.8	Relative size of the public sector	120

Acknowledgements

I want to thank my staff for their dedication at work and their assistance in some of the chapters in this book. In particular, Elaine Hung and Brenda Tang contributed to Chapter 5, Clara Lo contributed to Chapter 6 and Brenda Tang contributed to Chapter 7.

I am also indebted to Debby Ng for her assistance with organising some of the data and charts for the book and keeping my office life in order during the chaotic times when this book was being written. Without her help, I would not have been able to complete this book in such a timely fashion.

All economic data, data estimates and figures used in this book are created from the databank provided by CEIC Data Company Limited (CEIC). Founded in 1992 and acquired in 2005 by ISI Emerging Markets, CEIC has built its reputation on delivering accurate and comprehensive economic, industrial and financial data for economists globally. In particular, it has the most comprehensive economic research data on Asia and some of the emerging markets. CEIC implements meticulous measures to ensure the accuracy of its data, which is maintained by experienced researchers who aggregate data from close to 2,000 primary sources.

Preface

The subprime crisis has swept through global economies and financial systems like a devastating earthquake (a credit quake, as it is sometimes called in Europe) or tsunami (financial tsunami, as it is commonly known in Asia). No one is spared. There is only a difference in the magnitude of the impact being felt in different regions. There have been many analyses on the subject since the crisis broke in late 2007. However, they have insufficiencies that this book seeks to fill, including, most crucially, a lack of integrated analysis on the subprime crisis from the Asian perspective, misunderstanding about the Asian and Chinese aspects of the subprime crisis, erroneous views on the nature of the crisis, ignorance of Asia's contribution to the root of the subprime crisis, and erroneous analysis of the macro policy impact on the global system in the aftermath of the crisis.

There are many lessons that can be drawn from the subprime crisis, but they have not been systematically addressed, perhaps because everyone has been busy 'fighting the fire'. There are also significant implications of the crisis on the regulatory, macroeconomic and financial fronts in the post-crisis era. China certainly has a lot to learn, as it had just started financial liberalisation, for the insurance sector in particular, before this global crisis hit. Many people seem to remain overly optimistic that the crisis will be followed by a normal economic recovery so that our life can get back to normal.

This is no normal crisis, and hence, in my view, there is no normal post-crisis recovery. There were huge economic imbalances built up in the 1990s and early 2000s, all financed by massive debt in the developed world. The advent of financial derivatives, thanks to de-regulation, had only made these imbalances, and, hence, the ensuing crisis, more complicated. To unwind these imbalances from the web of complicated financial instruments spread throughout the world will take a long time. The loss of public confidence only adds difficulty to finding a solution. Hence, we may be in for a long post-bubble economic adjustment which will last for some years and feature de-leveraging and asset price deflation. World economic growth may experience a structural downward shift for the next decade, if not longer, and goods price inflation will remain subdued for some years. The economic black hole created by the deflationary forces of the subprime crisis is so big that even aggressive monetary easing, in the form of quantitative easing, by the global authorities may not necessarily bring back inflation in two to three years after the crisis is over.

The world is still complacent about these potential post-crisis events. The stock market, for example, is still trying to discount an economic recovery after the dust has settled. As a result, many investors are hoping for a market rebound after the crisis, as earnings growth resumes. What if there is no recovery, but just sub-par growth for a few years after the economy hits bottom? In this case, the economy (hence earnings growth momentum) will not move in a normal recession–recovery cycle, but instead in a recession-flat (or an L-shape, as some analysts call it) growth scenario. In this case, the stock market discounting a normal cyclical recovery will be wrong. It will be repeatedly disappointed because earnings growth will disappoint investors in an L-shape economic scenario. Time will tell whether this scenario will play out. But this is one possible outcome to which the world has not paid enough attention.

From Asia's and China's perspectives, despite their relatively stronger economic fundamentals, they will not be able to escape from the post-crisis impact, and they cannot afford to be complacent. The export-led growth model is shattered, but Asia has not changed fast enough to take on the new post-subprime paradigm. The whole of Asia is going through financial deregulation, especially China, which is putting serious effort into liberalising its insurance sector and is considering developing financial derivatives markets for insurance products. There is a danger that this global crisis might send the wrong signals about financial deregulation and deter liberalisation in Asia. So what are the regulatory lessons to be learned from the crisis, from the collapses of financial giants such as AIG, Lehman Brothers and Fortis? What are the macroeconomic policy lessons to be learned? What is life after Subprime going to be like?

We will definitely live in a different world – with less debt, higher savings and more regulations – after the post-bubble adjustment has worked itself through. There is a real possibility that global economic growth will suffer a structural downward shift in the coming years due to 'destructive creation' inflicted by financial innovation. This is a clear negative shock to the world economy, as opposed to the benign 'creative destruction' stemming from non-financial innovation, which is a positive shock for stimulating growth. The rest of the book provides some food for thought in the post-subprime paradigm.

Chi Lo

Introduction

It is an amazing coincidence that the US subprime crisis, which has swept the world into an unprecedented turmoil, happened exactly ten years after the Asian crisis. In July 1997, the Asian crisis broke in Thailand and then spread to the rest of Asia. In July 2007, US investment bank Bear Stearns disclosed that its two subprime hedge funds had lost nearly all of their value amid a rapid decline in the market for subprime mortgages. The revelation set off the subprime crisis, which spread throughout the world in the following months.

The epicentre of this crisis has changed, of course, from Asia to Europe and the USA. The buzzwords have also changed, from currency pegs, excessive corporate borrowing and foreign debt in the Asian crisis to securitisation, subprime mortgages and collateral debt obligations in the subprime crisis. However, the causes and symptoms of the subprime crisis are quite similar to those of the Asian crisis. So to say that the subprime crisis is an unexpected shock is a denial of human mistakes. Each crisis was preceded by a prolonged period of low interest rates leading to moral hazard, imprudent lending, regulatory oversight, excessive investment, and asset bubbles. After the subprime crisis broke, investors panicked on the back of soaring counterparty risk and plunging asset valuations. That triggered a credit crunch and pushed the US banking system towards insolvency; exactly what happened to Asia in the Asian crisis.

Greed is prevalent in both the subprime and Asian crises. Before the Asian crisis, massive foreign capital inflows to the region significantly boosted bank lending and corporate borrowing. Foreign investors were attracted by Asia's high-yield securities in the blind

1

faith that the regional currency pegs would hold forever and robust economic growth would support Asian corporates' repayment ability forever. Similarly, massive capital inflows flooded the USA and financed its huge current account deficit, fuelling excessive demand for credit and mortgage loans. The latter were repackaged into mortgage-backed securities (MBS) and other credit derivatives, like collateralised debt obligations (CDO). Investors outside the USA were attracted by the high yields of these structured products in the blind faith that the underlying parties all had AAA credit ratings.

Imprudence follows greed. Ten years ago, the Asians indulged in imprudent lending to corporates based on relationship and to mega projects and property development of dubious nature. Due diligence and commercial viability were totally ignored. In the subprime crisis, imprudence is seen in the proliferation of subprime mortgage loans and the so-called *ninja* loans (no income, no jobs and no assets for backing).

Indeed, easy credit made available by investor (and regulatory) imprudence was the root cause of creating asset bubbles in both crises. According to the so-called Minsky financial instability hypothesis (Minsky, 1992), strong and prolonged economic growth tends to produce complacency and, thus, imprudence and over-leveraging in the economy. There are three kinds of borrowers in the Minsky world, according to their repayment abilities. First is the hedge borrower, who can pay principal and interest from cash flow. Second is the speculative borrower, who can only pay interest and needs to roll over the principal by borrowing further. Third is the Ponzi borrower, who can pay neither interest nor principal and must borrow (or sell assets) just to meet the interest bill. Prolonged and robust economic growth typically increases the number of speculative and Ponzi borrowers, according to the Minsky hypothesis. They are the culprits who cause asset bubbles, which eventually burst with devastating economic results. The surge in subprime loans in the USA was a reflection of the dominance of the speculative and Ponzi borrowers.

In essence, irresponsible borrowers and imprudent investments are just a manifestation of the moral hazard problem. Before the Asian crisis, many of the regional banking systems and mega projects appeared to enjoy de facto government guarantees. This encouraged banks to lend irresponsibly. Meanwhile, Asian banks and corporates borrowed in foreign currencies at low interest rates, on the assumption that the regional pegged exchange rates would never change (Krugman, 1998 and Lo, 2003, Chapter 1). In this US subprime crisis, investors and banks used short-term funds to invest in long-term and complex structured financial derivatives, such as MBS and CDOs, on the assumption that the repayment ability of the underlying parties was unquestionable. These investors and banks also thought that they could have unlimited access to the interbank and money markets to roll over their funding on the assumption that the monetary authorities would bail out the markets.

Finally, there is a conflict of interest problem, which often takes the form of a principal–agent problem. In the Asian crisis, bank managers just ignored shareholders and public interest and lent indiscriminately to companies and projects under political or influential business pressure. Corruption to fatten the bank managers' own pockets only aggravated the problem. In the US subprime crisis, investors in MBS and CDOs expected mortgage lenders and banks to keep their credit standards. But in the 'originate and distribute' model, in which the mortgage lenders and banks originate the loans and sell them off at once, they had little incentive to scrutinise and keep the credit standards. Typically, mortgage lenders made the loans and at once sold them off to banks. The banks, in turn, securitised them and sold them off to investors throughout the world. The banks aimed at maximising only their fee income from securitisation but not the interest income from the loans. So they had the incentive to securitise and push the products off their books as soon as possible. Credit standards dropped sharply in the process, and no-one had any clues about the ultimate ownership of the underlying loans. So, when the US housing bubble burst, defaults surged, setting off a domino effect on the mortgage derivative instruments and shattering public confidence in the banking system as a whole.

Hence, those who argue that the subprime crisis was a 'black swan' event are either naïve or in denial. Despite numerous analyses of the subprime crisis, its causes and impact are still misread in many cases, especially from the Asian perspective. The plan of the book to address these insufficiencies is as follows.

Chapter 1 seeks to look at the basics of the subprime crisis, such as the origins of the subprime loans and the process by which they accumulated into such a gigantic problem, which has spread throughout the world economy. It gives a condensed analysis of the global crisis by focusing on the crux of the problems and eschewing the peripheral information which has been dealt with by other research.

Chapter 2 looks at the subprime crisis from an Asian perspective and argues that, contrary to many analysts' views, the crisis was not a 'black swan' event. Instead, it is a man-made event, which can be traced back to Asia and the global saving–investment imbalance. It argues that, in the post-subprime crisis period, banking will be a boring business with fancy financial derivatives gone. This is a controversial argument and I hope it will stimulate further research on the subject. Finally, it highlights the danger of the crisis sending the wrong signals to the Asian regulators on financial deregulation.

Chapter 3 examines the subprime impact on China. It argues that, although the financial impact of the crisis might not be large, its real impact from external demand implosion would be larger than expected. The latter point challenges the conventional wisdom that China is pretty much shielded from the external financial shock. Government ownership and heavy regulation of the Chinese banking system and a closed capital account have become blessings in disguise for China because they help limit, though not eliminate, the impact of the financial tsunami. Together with stronger economic fundamentals, these blessings will help China to recover first from the subprime crisis.

Chapter 4 analyses the macroeconomic implications of the subprime crisis. The first part deals with the implications for the world of China's role in the global crisis and refutes the naïve view that China will be able to save the world in the aftermath of the crisis. In fact, China suffers from some policy missteps that have constrained its growth potential. The second part discusses the lessons for China's economic policy and banking sector risks in the post-crisis world. It also highlights the risk of a slowdown in Sino-western cooperation in building a modern Chinese banking system.

Chapter 5 gives a rundown on the global policy responses to the subprime crisis. It examines the differences between the Asian 'cool' policy response to the crisis and the developed world's rigorous reaction. The discussion points out the flaws in the authorities' rescue efforts and suggests a plausible way out of the financial mess. It also argues that it would be better for China to heed the lessons now and make a good start on its financial deregulation efforts rather than jumping into financial engineering and excessive consumerism and ending up with another big financial mess to clean up in the future.

Chapter 6 looks at AIG's collapse, which has significant micro relevance to drawing regulatory lessons for the insurance industry in China, which is in the middle of de-regulating its financial sector and considering the development of a domestic credit derivatives market as part of the financial modernisation programme. In particular, we will look at the regulatory loopholes that allowed AIG to stray away from its core business and finally triggered its failure. The moral of the story is that risk control is of utmost importance to insurance companies and they must not be tempted to maximise short-term profit as a business strategy. If mismanaged, the good intention of financial engineering could turn out to be detrimental to the corporate and financial sectors, or even the whole economy.

Chapter 7 looks at the collapse of Lehman Brothers and Fortis, which has crucial macro relevance to drawing policy lessons for the banking sectors and regulators in the coming years in China as well as in the developed world. It argues that the influence of universal banks will grow in the post-subprime era, which will bode well for the Chinese banking/financial conglomerate model when it comes to overseas expansion. The discussion also highlights the devastating result of financial innovation in the form of 'destructive creation', which is a negative shock to the economy, as opposed to the benign effect of non-financial innovation in the form of 'creative destruction', which is a positive shock.

Chapter 8 focuses on the macro policy response of the developed world to save the global system from imploding. One of the hotly debated policies being used is 'quantitative easing'. I argue here, contrary to the views of many others, that quantitative easing would not cause inflation in the next few years. The chapter also assesses the situation in China, which has its own particular version of 'quantitative easing'. The Japanese experience, in its failure in using quantitative easing to save its economy, is not only relevant to the US policymakers when conducting anti-crisis policy; it also reveals a different but very crucial challenge for the Chinese authorities. And that is not to let deflationary expectations take hold. Contrary to the common perception that China has a high inflation tendency, I argue that the deflation risk in China is more serious than in the

US, which makes the experience of Japan's failed quantitative easing policy more important to heed.

Chapters 9 and 10 conclude with my projection of the global economy's life after the subprime crisis. Chapter 9 focuses on the adjustment that Asia will go through and the economic and investment environment in the years to come. The discussion highlights the danger of capital protectionism, which arguably is the worst form of protectionism. This is because, unlike trade protectionism, which hurts specific goods, capital protectionism destroys every ingredient of globalisation in one stroke. The discussion also assesses the fear that China may massively shift out of its US dollar assets in the post-subprime years and cause another wave of the financial crisis.

Chapter 10 argues that China will see two development trends emerge in the post-subprime world: the rise of the Chinese consumer to shift the growth structure of the Chinese economy, and increase in government intervention in the domestic economy. The structural shift to a consumer-led economy will not be easy, because there are political and structural obstacles to the change. The argument highlights the risk of rising political tension, often manifested in trade and capital protectionism, between China and the crisis-hit western world. The other potential risk, of increasing government intervention, will have little noticeable impact in the short term. But, beyond the subprime crisis, whether or not China continues with further economic liberalisation will have profound implications on the country's long-term growth outlook and asset values.

1
The Basics of the 'Financial Tsunami'

The US subprime crisis was rooted in a combination of financial deregulation and monetary policy oversight amid two decades of financial liberalisation in the 1980s and 1990s. Financial deregulation backfired and was manifest in twenty years of risky practices in lending and borrowing, securitisation of home loans and regulatory oversight. The bursting of the US housing bubble triggered the subprime crisis and spread it across the world. Securitisation on the back of loose regulations allowed banks to broadly distribute risks to investors, including banks, individuals, financial firms and hedge funds, who eventually suffered significant losses when mortgage payment defaults soared.

As the subprime-induced credit crunch pulled down asset prices indiscriminately, what was at first a liquidity crisis soon turned into a solvency crisis for individual banks, prompting the global authorities to employ radical measures such as partial bank nationalisation, troubled-asset purchases and other forms of direct market interventions to contain the 'credit quake' or 'financial tsunami', as it is called in Asia. Asia's policy response has remained relatively calm in this subprime debacle because it has learnt good lessons from the 1997/98 Asian crisis. The spirit and essence of these lessons are also relevant to the Chinese authorities, who are in the middle of liberalising China's insurance industry and considering the development of a domestic credit derivatives market.

From subprime to securitisation ...

The word 'subprime' in relation to mortgages in the USA generally refers to those mortgages targeted at borrowers with impaired

or low credit ratings and low income level who may find it difficult to obtain finance through traditional sources, such as Prime
mortgages and Alt-A. Subprime borrowers have the highest per-
ceived default risk, as compared with Prime and Alt-A borrowers.
In essence, subprime borrowers are those who have a history of
loan delinquency or default, those with a record of bankruptcy,
and those with low income levels relative to their mortgage payment ability.

Traditionally, banks lent money to homeowners for their mortgages and kept the risk of default, called credit risk, on their balance
sheets. It is obvious that banks would not issue much mortgage debt
to high-risk borrowers unless they could transfer the risks and earn
higher yields at the same time. With the advent of securitisation,
they can do just that. Banks can transfer credit risk in the property
market to investors through mortgage-backed securities (MBS) and
collateralised debt obligations (CDOs). These financial derivatives
effectively allow banks to sell the mortgage payments rights and
related credit risk to investors anywhere in the world. This, in turn,
means that the underlying credit risk of the MBS and CDOs can be
broadly distributed to investors, hedge funds and financial firms,

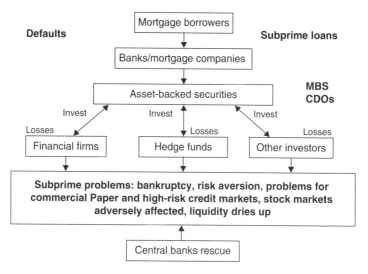

Chart 1.1   Anatomy of the subprime crisis

both in the USA and in other parts of the world. Chart 1.1 provides a simple anatomy of the subprime problem.

... to the 'financial tsunami' (or 'credit quake')

The securitisation process went well between 2001, when the IT bubble burst, and late 2007, when the subprime crisis broke. The Fed slashed interest rates and kept them low for a long time to help the economy through the post-IT-bubble adjustment process (Chart 1.2). In those years with declining and low interest rates, many banks earned higher yields by buying MBS, CDOs and other mortgage-related derivatives in an environment of low credit risk premium and few loan defaults. Meanwhile, with lax lending standards and rising housing prices, subprime borrowers could easily get access to credit to buy homes and quickly refinance their mortgages on more favourable terms.

Banks with a strong credit rating were able to take on debt at low interest rates. So they borrowed by issuing short-dated bonds or commercial papers, invested the proceeds in the high-yield MBS and CDOs and pocketed the yield difference as profits. This balance-sheet mismatch strategy (by borrowing short and investing long) magnified their profits during the falling interest rate housing boom

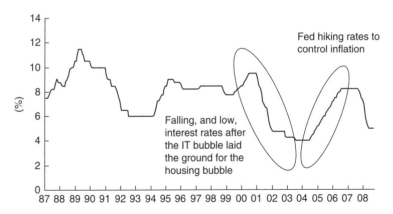

Chart 1.2   US prime lending rate
Source: CEIC.

period, but inflicted large losses when the interest rate cycle turned in 2005.

When the Fed tried to rein in inflation in 2005, interest rates began to rise and housing prices started to drop, making refinancing more difficult. To make matters worse, most of the subprime mortgages were adjustable rate mortgages (ARM). This meant that subprime borrowers had to repay interest according to the rising market interest rates. As a result, mortgage delinquency and foreclosure rates rose sharply, as easy initial terms expired, home prices failed to go up as anticipated, and ARM interest rates were reset higher.

Moreover, instead of reselling the MBS and CDOs to other investors, many banks retained significant amounts of these derivatives on their books. When the housing bubble burst, mortgage payment defaults soared, pulling down sharply the market value of the MBS and CDOs. Banks were unable to sell these investments as market liquidity dried up. Individual investors, financial firms and hedge funds holding MBS and CDOs faced the same situation. All suffered significant losses as a result.

The subprime woes soon led to a wholesale collapse in confidence in the financial system, pushing the worries about counterparty risk to the extreme. This created a severe credit crunch, referred to as a 'credit quake' in the developed markets and a 'financial tsunami' in Asia, which pulled down asset prices indiscriminately. Hence, what was at first a liquidity crisis soon turned into a solvency crisis for individual banks.

Europe affected, but Asia stood firm

The US subprime crisis was quickly transmitted to Europe, as the European banks were some of the largest holders of the US mortgage-related derivative instruments. During the good times, they loaded up the MBS and CDOs with cheap USD funding. But when the subprime crisis broke, USD funding sources of all sorts, including money market funds, bank depositors and other investors, withdrew cash *en masse*. European banks soon found their funding increasingly difficult and expensive to replace. When the credit market eventually seized up after the failure of Lehman Brothers in September 2008, the domino effect was quickly felt in Europe, pulling down big banks like Fortis and HBOS and forcing them into government hands for rescue.

When the financial contagion hit Asia, it wreaked havoc in the regional financial and currency markets, even though the regional banks had very limited exposure to the subprime toxic assets. However, the overall impact on the regional financial system was relatively small. Asia's strong fundamentals, including large current account surpluses, huge foreign reserves, low foreign debts and high savings rates, have helped shield its financial systems from the 'financial tsunami'. However, the region's heavy reliance on export-led growth has significantly pushed its economies deep into recession as global demand contracts under the weight of the post-bubble adjustment in the developed world.

Nevertheless, Asia's financial strength today is a reflection of the lessons it learned from the 1997/98 Asian crisis: do not liberalise the financial sector hastily; borrow in moderation; save in earnest; develop a strong economy and invest in productivity. As far as regulation is concerned, Asia has also not reduced the role of the government as much as the USA because, as former US Fed chairman Alan Greenspan acknowledged in 2008, financial institutions cannot self-regulate. The virtue of Adam Smith's invisible hand in the market has to be balanced by the 'visible hand' of the government implementing responsible and sensible regulatory control.

On the whole, the subprime crisis caused panic in the global financial markets and resulted in a complete loss of confidence, turning what was originally a liquidity squeeze into solvency crises. The most noteworthy was the bankruptcy of Lehman Brothers, followed by Merrill Lynch and AIG in the USA, Fortis in Europe and HBOS in the UK, to name just a few. The sharp worsening of the crisis in September and October 2008 eventually prompted the global authorities to employ radical measures such as concerted interest rate cuts, quantitative easing, partial bank nationalisation, troubled-asset purchases and other forms of direct market interventions to control financial tsunami. The outbreak of the crisis, its impact on the financial system and regulatory response are all important lessons which will be relevant in the future to the global regulators and financial institutions' business practice and operation models.

The seed of the subprime crisis

There is excellent and detailed work published on the subprime crisis analysis (Read, 2009; Shiller, 2008; Zandi, 2008). But here is my condensed analysis as a lead to our discussion of the crisis from a different perspective for the rest of the book. In my view, financial deregulation and monetary policy oversight during the twenty years of financial liberalisation in the 1980s and 1990s were a lethal combination for creating the subprime crisis. The global major central banks, the US Federal Reserve, the Bank of England and the European Central Bank in particular, had run an overly loose monetary policy in a dynamic, entrepreneurial, globalised and capitalist system, and ended up turning the original good economic policy intention into the seed of another shocking crisis. But that did not mean that capitalism had failed. Rather, the subprime crisis was a result of regulatory failure in the capitalist system.

Entrepreneurship and risk-taking lie at the heart of the capitalist system, driving economic agents to maximise the expected rate of investment return. The logic of more entrepreneurship meaning higher productivity in the economy has dominated modern central bank thinking. But many central bankers in the developed world also tended to view accelerating productivity growth as a one-sided positive in that it raises the expected rate of investment return with little risk of economic overheating. Hence, they thought that monetary policy did not need to be tightened up when there was fast productivity growth.

The problem with this line of thinking is that, if real interest rate does not rise along with the expected rate of return, asset bubbles, moral hazard and Ponzi games will emerge. Financial deregulation under such circumstances only makes asset bubbles and excess demand more severe. This was what happened in the latter half of the 1990s, when rapid productivity growth in the USA (thanks to technological advancement) emerged alongside intensifying financial deregulation.

Firms will invest more when their expected rate of investment return rises. But not all firms' projects are good and viable. So a rise in the real interest rate will help weed out bad investments and allocate resources to the most efficient areas and firms over time. If the real rate does not rise, excessive and inefficient investments will result. Financial deregulation and regulatory oversight only aggravate the excess problem by misallocating credit, distorting intertemporal choice and, thus, bringing too much future spending to the present. This, in turn, creates asset and demand bubbles. When the bubbles eventually go bust, investment collapses as firms finally come to terms with the unsustainable economic and financial excesses.

After the US IT bubble burst in late 2000, the Fed responded by slashing interest rates and keeping them low for a long time. While the move seemed justified to prevent the economic shock from setting off a downward spiral at the time, it also had the unintended impact of creating a breeding ground for the next (housing) bubble. The Fed's aggressive monetary easing prevented the post-IT-bubble liquidation process from taking place, hence exacerbating the problem of bringing too much spending forward from the future. The excess was channeled to overconsumption, as seen in the worsening US current account deficit (Chart 1.3), and the housing market. The housing bubble finally burst when the Fed started raising interest rates in 2005 and 2006 (see Chart 1.2), triggering the subprime crisis.

The US monetary policy was not the only problem. The creation in 1999 of the Euro zone, which centralised monetary policies of the member countries into one European Central Bank (ECB), also played a crucial role in creating the global credit bubble. Monetary union eliminates currency risk but not credit risk. With only one currency, the euro, and one monetary policy, credit spreads in some Euroland countries should have risen to reflect their underlying

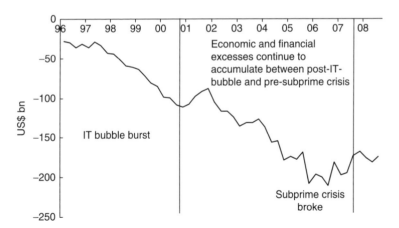

Chart 1.3 US current account deficit
Source: CEIC.

risks. But the ECB, in an attempt to ensure 'stability' in the early days of the euro, had kept an overly loose monetary policy for a long time. Thus, asset bubbles, fuelled by easy credit, emerged especially in the peripheral, smaller, Euroland countries, such as Ireland, Spain, Greece and Portugal.

Across the Atlantic, Asia also played a crucial role in fuelling the economic and financial excesses in the developed world. Indeed, there are similarities between the symptoms in the run-up to the 1997/98 Asian crisis and the 2007/08 subprime crisis. Chapter 2 deals with this subject.

2
The Asian Relevance to the Subprime Crisis

The 1997/98 Asian crisis and the 2007/08 subprime crisis have many similarities. But do not expect the western world to stage a fast recovery from the subprime crisis as Asia did from the Asian crisis. The post-subprime crisis adjustment will be about asset deflation and de-leveraging, which will last for years. Some economists even see the possibility of a return of depression-like economic problems, which dominated the world economy in the 1930s, after the financial tsunami (for example, see Krugman, 2009). Re-regulation of the developed world banking sector means that a plain vanilla banking model will return and sophisticated financial engineering practice will be gone for a long time. Medium-term global growth will experience a structural downward shift, unless the developing world raises consumption sharply. But this is unlikely to happen, as the saving habits of the developing nations, especially Asia, will not change so easily. The fall in consumption in the developed world will put an end to the emerging markets' export-led development model, crimping profit growth in Asia's export-led economies and sectors in the coming years.

Not a black swan event

Some analysts argue that the current subprime crisis is a '*black swan*' event. The term *black swan* comes from the ancient western concept that all swans are white. In that context, a black swan was a metaphor for something that could not exist (Taleb, 2007). Ever since black swans were discovered in Australia in the seventeenth century, the term *black swan* has been used to connote the actual happening of a highly unlikely event with unprecedented and devastating effects. I disagree. The subprime crisis itself is not a *black swan* event, though the resultant credit crunch and confidence crisis may qualify. This is because all the events and factors leading up to the current crisis were known.

From a macro perspective, the Asian crisis and the subprime debacle have similarities in their causes and symptoms – namely a prolonged period of low interest rates leading to moral hazard, imprudent lending, regulatory oversight, excessive investment, and asset bubbles. But the advent of financial derivatives has made today's subprime crisis more complicated.

The US current account deficit ballooned to above the crisis threshold of 5% of GDP before the subprime crisis broke, just as in Asia before the 1997/98 financial crisis (Chart 2.1). Notably, Thailand, where the Asian crisis started, had a current account deficit of over 8% of GDP prior to the crisis; the USA had a current account deficit of 6% in the year before the subprime crisis!

The Americans have gone into a debt-financed spending spree for over a decade, pushing the loan-to-deposit ratio in the banking system to over 100%. Everything from personal consumption to financial investment has been funded by debts. The blow-out in the US loan-to-deposit ratio recalls vividly the situation in Asia prior

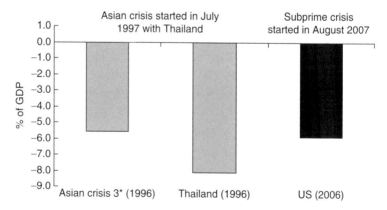

Chart 2.1   Current account balances before crisis
Note: * Average of Korea, Indonesia, Thailand.
Source: CEIC.

to the regional crisis (Chart 2.2). While Asia financed its excessive spending by foreign borrowing, so have the Americans (Chart 2.3). Foreign debts in both America and the three Asian crisis countries that needed IMF bailout (Korea, Thailand and Indonesia) all soared before their respective crises.

Gross US foreign debt is even bigger than in the Asian crisis countries. However, nearly all of America's foreign liabilities are

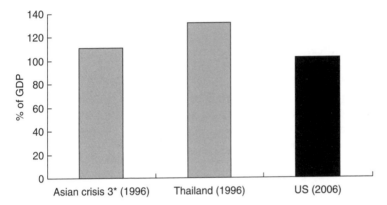

Chart 2.2   Loan-to-deposit ratios before crisis
Note: * Average of Korea, Indonesia, Thailand.
Source: CEIC.

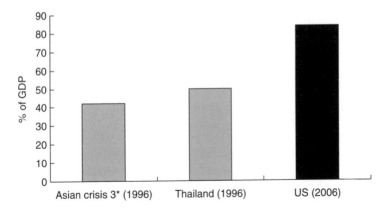

Chart 2.3   Foreign debt before crisis
Note: * Average of Korea, Indonesia, Thailand.
Source: CEIC.

denominated in USD, due mainly to the USD's reserve currency and international trade status. Moreover, the US government still enjoys strong international confidence in its debt servicing and repayment ability. Hence, the USA has not suffered a sudden seizure of capital inflow, and there has not been a USD crisis. This is quite different from the Asian crisis, when massive capital outflow caused a regional currency crisis alongside the financial crisis.

The Asian connection

Behind these economic and financial excesses there is an Asian connection. First, shiploads of cheap goods from Asia, notably China, helped keep US inflation down. This prompted the Americans, and the Fed, to think that they could spend lavishly without igniting inflation at the same time. Second, over $4.3 trillion foreign reserves in Asian central banks, combined with billions of petrodollars from the Middle East, provided the USA with enormous liquidity. This was mostly poured into US Treasury and mortgage-backed securities, suppressing US bond yields, inflating the housing bubble and encouraging excessive US household borrowing to fund consumption.

Asia's high savings also created ample liquidity and cheap credit for enhancing western banks' and speculators' leveraging power to fuel the global asset bubbles. Through carry trades, these international players borrowed at low Asian, especially Japanese, interest rates and swapped the proceeds into high-yield currencies and markets. In a nutshell, frugal Asians, with the Chinese and Japanese accounting for over 40% of the world's central bank reserves, have lived below their means with savings flowing westwards to allow the spendthrift Americans to live beyond their means. While it lasted, this cross-Atlantic saving–spending mischief became a stable disequilibrium, enabling Asia to supercharge growth by lending to America so that it could buy Asian exports. As the party ends with the subprime crisis, Asia will be suffering too in the post-bubble adjustment period in the coming years as the financial excess implodes. Indeed, despite its stronger economic fundamentals and financial foundation than the western world this time around, Asia has not learnt from the 1997/98 regional crisis that overreliance on export-led growth is an unsustainable long-term growth model (see Chapter 9).

The adjustment

The deepening of the US subprime crisis after September 2008, despite the Fed's repeated massive liquidity injection, shows that the markets had failed to clear on their own and the global financial system had stalled. There would be two possible outcomes of the crisis – either a global financial meltdown or a full-scale government bailout. History and the government actions suggest the latter.

Forced consolidation, with numerous bank failures, will last for some years in the post-subprime crisis period. In the US Savings & Loans (S&L) crisis back in the late 1980s and early 1990s, over 1,000 US banks failed. In this crisis so far, at the time of writing, only a couple of hundred US banks have failed. And the subprime crisis is a much bigger shock than the S&L crisis. Further, US bank lending to non-financial firms had only started to slow down in 2008, a year after the subprime crisis broke (Chart 2.4). All these suggest that the adjustment process was still in an early stage. Outright contraction in bank lending would be an essential part of the cleansing process. The long process of declining bank credit and bank retrenchment will hurt economic growth for some years, as bank credit goes to support real corporate and consumer spending while non-bank credit

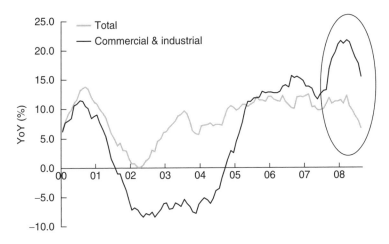

Chart 2.4   US bank loan growth
Source: CEIC.

(by those investment banks) goes to finance portfolio investment and does not affect real spending directly.

The situation in Europe is worse, due to the ECB's inflexible monetary policy and delay in responding to the crisis until late 2008. Monetary policy aside, it seems that a bank nationalisation process had begun earlier in Europe than in the USA to tackle the crisis. But the lack of a central financial regulator and treasury has continued to hinder Europe's ability to implement a coherent crisis response and forced the European countries to adopt a case-by-case approach in addressing this financial crisis.

If unaltered, this short-term fix in Europe will have long-term negative implications. Not only is it expensive, but it also protects bad banks at the expense of the good ones. Delaying the process of forcing weak banks to close will only slow the normalisation of lending and encourages moral hazard, which could be even more costly to taxpayers down the road. In fact, this mentality of forbearance is prevalent among the global authorities in their crisis bailout strategy (see below).

In these days, bailouts are deemed necessary for only one reason: to stabilise the financial sector in a crisis of contagion. They are intended to protect the integrity of the whole financial system, so the logic goes. However, bailouts do not guarantee a true recovery in the financial markets (much less an economic recovery). Bailouts also do not reduce investor uncertainty or investor risk aversion. This is because bailouts change the nature of the underlying market/ economic risks to the investor, with the proportion of 'endogenous' (or systemic) risk rising relative to 'exogenous' (or systematic) risk. In the asset market's perspective, this means that, even though asset prices may be very cheap on the basis of conventional valuation metrics, the higher 'endogenous' or systemic nature of risk makes the future direction of asset prices unpredictable. In short, not only is the total risk of investment rising in this financial climate, but the nature of the underlying risk has become more adverse than before.

As and when global confidence returns and risk aversion fades, the authorities should shift away from bailouts towards foreclosures of bad banks. Foreclosures will lay the foundation for the financial market and economic recovery. First, foreclosures reliquefy the economy in a general equilibrium 'bottom-up' way, rather than as a 'top-down' macro policy stimulus. A bottom-up approach will be more effective as a post-subprime adjustment because the economic risks have tilted towards being endogenous in nature. Second, foreclosures tighten capacity utilisation (again via a 'bottom-up' process rather than as a 'top-down' macro stimulus). This will help rebuild rising price expectations to counteract the risk of price deflation in the post-crisis world.

These are the important microeconomic foundations for sustaining a macro economic recovery. Yet many policymakers in the world are ignoring this on the grounds of the need for stabilising the global crisis. The crisis will pass; the global economy will be stabilised eventually. The question is whether the global authorities will take the necessary pains – i.e. to foreclose the bad banks – to sustain the economic recovery, or will they just prefer to hide in their own local agendas and wait for the next, perhaps bigger, crisis to erupt so that they can provide the bailouts again?

The end game

While Asian growth experienced a V-shaped rebound a year after the 1997/98 Asian crisis, thanks to its young and vibrant economic structure and a quick return of confidence, don't bet on the same happening in Europe and the USA. Even if the US Troubled Asset Relief Programme (TARP) manages to turn confidence around and the European authorities finally wake up to reality and join in a concerted reflation/bailout effort, history shows that the post-bubble adjustment in developed economies will take a long time.

After the Resolution Trust Corp. was set up in 1989, it took almost a year for US stocks to bottom and two years for credit and economic conditions to normalise. In its 1992 financial crisis, the Swedish government also enforced a wholesale government bailout to guarantee all bank liabilities and recapitalise the banks, but the Swedish stock market and economy still took more than two years to recover. Japan was in an even worse position, as the set-up of the Financial Supervisory Agency in 1997 to clean up bank balance sheets did not help the economy recover until five years later; and some are still wondering if the economy ever did manage a true recovery.

Spendthrift debt-financed US consumers will have to retrench; the US current account deficit will have to continue to shrink to rebalance global saving and investment habits. Thrift will replace leverage throughout the developed world. The huge bailout costs also mean that taxes across Europe and America will rise in the coming years, further crimping consumption power. Global growth will experience a structural downward shift, unless the developing world raises consumption sharply. This looks unlikely in the short term, as the saving habit of the developing world, especially Asia, will not change so fast. Consumers worldwide will shift towards value from luxury spending, suggesting that mid-market goods and services providers will outperform luxury brands in the years to come.

The post-subprime crisis adjustment will be about asset deflation and de-leveraging, especially in the finance and household sectors in the developed world. This type of adjustment will last for years because it takes a long time for the financial sector to rebuild capital. The fall in consumption in the developed world will put an end to the emerging markets' export-led development model, which had supercharged their growth for over a decade, because external demand will be weak in the future. This also means that profit growth in the export-led economies and sectors will be constrained for years.

Re-regulating the banks

The subprime crisis is a man-made crisis, not a *black swan* event. Some economists even argued that the US government's actions and interventions, rather than any inherent failure or instability of the private sector, caused, prolonged and dramatically worsened the crisis (Taylor, 2009). To put right their mistakes in the coming years, regulators will not let banks securitise lending and shift it off their balance sheets to create new lending capacity so easily. The developed world's banking sector will become slimmer, less risky and less profitable. Money markets will also be smaller and more expensive, so that banks will have to rely more on the traditional funding source of deposits. A plain vanilla banking model of simple lending and borrowing will return; fancy derivatives will be gone.

When one considers the essence of the subprime crisis, this is not an overly pessimistic scenario for the post-crisis global banking environment. A modern economy cannot grow if its financial system is not operating effectively. Banks, along with the wider financial system, act as vital intermediaries allowing credit to flow from savers to borrowers with viable ventures. But the nature of the banking business rests on balance-sheet mismatch, whereby banks borrow short-term funds to make long-term loans. This, in turn, relies on public confidence in the banks.

But, despite the importance of the banks and the financial system, it is difficult to attribute the deep subprime-induced economic recessions in the developed world to a sudden drop in credit availability after the crisis in September and October 2008. That happened later. Instead, evidence shows that the shock from the bank failures, along with already strained economic conditions, shattered confidence and caused a sudden drop in global demand. At the same time as companies began retrenching and cutting investment spending, the financial system had been tightening credit supply due to a sharp rise in risk aversion. With falling sales and profitability on the back of the rising cost of borrowing (or an outright dearth of credit), corporate failures and defaults soared. That hurt confidence further, including among banks, which feared for both their own viability and counterparty risk. As a result, banks turned ultraconservative and stopped lending. The whole global system suffered as a result.

So the global authorities are determined to break the credit logjam and the downward economic spiral. In all countries, monetary policy has been loosened to repair confidence and encourage risk-taking. The USA has even taken the lead, stretching its monetary easing to the extreme by pursuing 'quantitative easing' (see Chapter 8), and using public money to buy assets outright to ease the credit flow. Japan, which implemented quantitative easing between 2001 and 2006, and other major banks followed suit.

In this attempt to tackle the subprime crisis, the global authorities have sought to reduce the uncertainties over bank balance sheets by transferring risks from the banks to the public sector. While this is a fire-fighting measure, it is not a long-term solution. Foreclosures and re-regulation are the necessary micro steps to ensure the return of sound banking systems (see above). Banking is fundamentally a dangerous business. This danger had been intensified over the past twenty years due to too much de-regulation on the back of intensifying competition (see Chapter 7).

Don't send the wrong message

Thus, to correct their mistakes, banks will have to become more boring, generating less profit from fancy financial engineering, and more heavily regulated relative to the past two decades. Granted, restrictions will hurt economic opportunities and profitability in the next economic upswing, but it will be a small price to pay for greater protection from another, perhaps bigger, banking crisis in the future.

However, the regulatory implications for Asia are different. From a policy perspective, the danger of the subprime crisis and the subsequent re-regulation of the global banks is that they may send a wrong signal to Asian regulators that financial innovation is bad and government control is good, as the restrictive Chinese model seems to have shown. A case in point is the rapid collapse of US investment bank Bear Sterns and UK mortgage lender Northern Rock. The former was at the forefront of financial innovation in the securities markets; the latter was lauded for its innovative funding strategy.

The correct message from these failures should be that Asia should ensure that any move away from traditional banking practices towards more innovative techniques is accompanied by enhanced risk management. It will be extremely unfortunate if the wrong message gets out and delays or even deters further financial liberalisation in the developing world. Asian regulators should take the subprime crisis lesson seriously to improve their regulatory systems. As Asian financial markets expand into new terrain, policymakers should put in place measures to deal with risks posed by financial innovation, but should not shy away from financial liberalisation or suppress financial innovation.

3
The Subprime Impact on China

The damaging financial effect of the subprime crisis on China and its banking system is limited: less than 1% of total assets in the system, according to the market estimation. Even the deepening of the crisis after US investment bank Lehman Brothers went broke in September 2008 did not inflict further damage on Chinese banks because they had been cutting foreign risk exposure way before the crisis. This limited impact was a result of government ownership, strict regulations and a closed capital account that have all added up to shield the Chinese financial system from the external shock. Hence, there was no confidence crisis and no counterparty risk in the Chinese banking system.

However, the real impact on the economy is much bigger than expected, due to the spillover effect of trade on domestic demand. Conventional wisdom is wrong when assessing the trade impact on China's growth. Some also fear that China might fall into a debt–deflation spiral, which would hurt its long-term economic growth and asset values in the post-subprime world. But that is unlikely, due to improvement in the Chinese banking and corporate sectors and under-leveraging in the consumer sector.

Chinese banks' subprime exposure

The worsening of the US subprime crisis, as seen in the failure of the 158-year-old investment bank Lehman Brothers and the nationalisation of Fannie Mae and Freddie Mac and AIG (America's largest insurance company) within three weeks in September 2008, had raised concerns about the stability of China's banking system. In particular, the worries were focused on the Chinese banks' exposure to Lehman Brothers' default and to the total subprime problem.

Market information at the end of 2008 (the latest data available at the time of writing) showed that the Chinese banks had very limited exposure to the US subprime crisis. Weighted average exposure of the seven largest Chinese commercial banks (Industrial and Commercial Bank of China (ICBC), Bank of China (BoC), China Construction Bank (CCB), China Merchant Bank (CMB), Industrial Bank, Citic Bank and Bank of Communications (BCom)) to Lehman's default amounts to only 0.02% of their total assets. Even if there were a 100% write-off of these bad assets, research from HSBC, a British bank, estimated that the Chinese banks' average net profit would only drop by 2.5% at most in 2008. Even if we include the US government mortgage agency debts, the Chinese banks' exposure to the total subprime (Lehman + agency) assets amounted to only 0.5% of their total assets (Table 3.1). From a macro perspective, Chinese banks have been reducing their foreign asset holdings in recent years (Chart 3.1), suggesting that they had been cutting foreign risk exposure. This was the biggest positive contributor to shielding the Chinese banking system from the impact of the subprime crisis.

Table 3.1   Chinese banks' exposure to the US subprime crisis (1H08)

	Lehman Brothers (US$ mn)	US govt agency debts (US$ mn)	Total (US$ mn)	Exposure to Lehman as % of total assets	Total subprime exposure as % of total assets
BOC	130	17,286	17,416	0.05	1.83
B.Comm	70	n/a	70	0.02	0.02
CCB	n/a	3,250	3,250	0.02	0.31
CITIC Bank	159	1,584	1,743	0.05	1.06
CMB	70	255	325	0.03	0.16
ICBC	152	2,716	2,868	0.01	0.21
Ind. Bank	34	0	34	0.02	0.02

Source: Company reports.

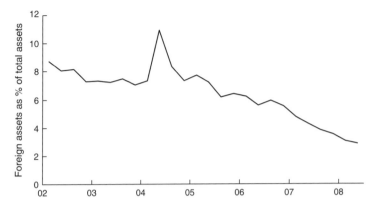

Chart 3.1 Chinese banks holding fewer foreign assets
Source: CEIC.

Banking sector fundamentals

China's banking system has been seen as the Achilles' heel of its economy due to the poor asset quality, lack of market discipline and opaque operation model. The banking industry is still heavily regulated; risk control systems are still defective and policy intervention still distorts the price of credit. Thus, much improvement is still needed. But this is not to deny that things have changed for the better in recent years. The government's recapitalisation efforts have worked with its public listing and foreign ownership strategies to improve the banking fundamentals, as seen in the steady decline in the banks' non-performing loans and increase in their capital–asset ratios (Chart 3.2).

Ironically, Chinese banks look more solid than their western counterparts on the back of the US subprime crisis. While the US banks have been lending aggressively and imprudently for over ten years, causing the banking system's loan-to-deposit ratio to explode, the Chinese banks have been scaling back lending activity (Chart 3.3). The fall in the Chinese loan-to-deposit ratio reflects both Beijing's credit control to rein in runaway growth in recent years and improvement in risk control among the Chinese banks. For example, in the mortgage loan business, the minimum down payment is 30% and the average mortgage loan life is less than twenty years. These are much more stringent

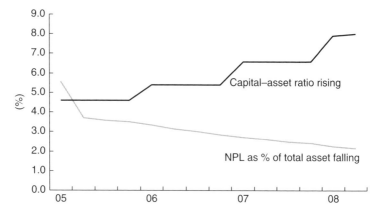

Chart 3.2   Improving Chinese bank asset quality
Source: CEIC.

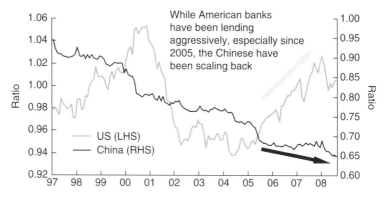

Chart 3.3   Loan-to-deposit ratios
Source: CEIC.

than the conditions in many developed markets. Rising competition among banks, public listing and foreign ownership have also brought in some market discipline to the Chinese banking sector.

Since all the major commercial banks are either directly or majority-owned by the government, this amounts to an implicit government guarantee of the banks and helps eliminate counterparty risk in the system. Hence, when the subprime crisis erupted, there was no

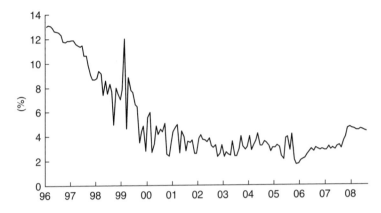

Chart 3.4   Three-month China interbank offered rate (CHIBOR)
Source: CEIC.

confidence crisis and no disruption of credit flow in the Chinese banking system as there was in the developed world. The stability of the Chinese system can be seen in the low and stable Chinese interbank rates throughout the subprime crisis (Chart 3.4).

From a systemic risk perspective, the Chinese banks are by default safer than their western counterparts because of government ownership, heavy regulations and their unsophistication, which bar them from getting involved in highly leveraged investments and product development. China's closed capital account, which bars free flow of portfolio capital, and heavily controlled banking system mean that its banks are insulated from the global financial turmoil.

Crisis prompts policy shift

Before the subprime crisis, Beijing was unclear about its monetary policy stance because, although economic momentum was slowing, inflation remained a concern. However, the deepening of the subprime crisis and the significant damage it was causing to global aggregate demand conditions acted as a catalyst in dispelling Beijing's inflation concerns and prompting it to move into monetary easing with conviction in late 2008. This should help improve the Chinese banking environment in the post-subprime economic adjustment environment in the coming years.

The weakest link in the economy is the export sector, which is exposed to the global demand cycle. China's growth momentum slowed sharply in 2008 when net exports became a negative contributor to (i.e. a drag on) GDP growth (Chart 3.5). Meanwhile, the RMB's real effective exchange rate had gone up sharply (Chart 3.6), adding to concerns about a significant spillover effect from the

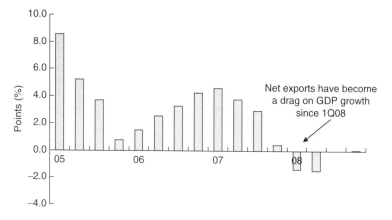

Chart 3.5   Net exports' contribution to nominal GDP growth
Source: CEIC.

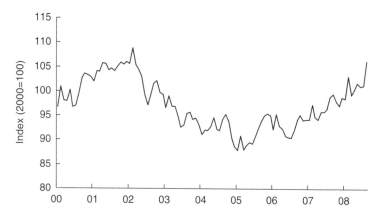

Chart 3.6   RMB real effective exchange rate
Source: CEIC.

export damages to the domestic sector. All macro indicators, including industrial output, the Purchasing Manager Index, investment and energy output, had plunged in the second half of 2008. Inflationary pressures had also subsided significantly, with CPI inflation slowing from over 8% at its peak rate in early 2008 to about 1% by year-end. Arguably, the US subprime crisis has aggravated and exposed China's economic weakness and, thus, given the Chinese authorities a clear signal to end their three-year economic tightening policy and switch to policy easing to contain the economic damages from the external shock.

The bigger-than-expected real impact

Indeed, although the financial impact of the subprime crisis on China is limited, its real impact on the economy is larger than expected. This is because conventional analysis has often overlooked the spill-over impact of trade on domestic investment and job growth. This impact is big enough to affect over half of investment spending and urban employment, according to my estimate. The conventional wisdom is that China's push for market diversification in recent years will help reduce the impact of weaker demand from the developed markets. But the conventional wisdom is wrong because it ignores

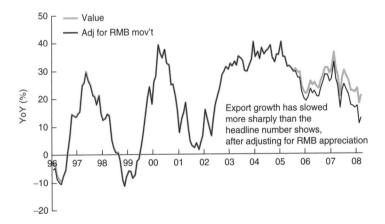

Chart 3.7   China's export growth
Source: CEIC.

the spillover effect of exports on China's domestic investment and job growth (see below).

In addition to weakening external demand, the rising RMB exchange rate is hurting China's export growth more than the data tell us. Adjusted for RMB appreciation, China's export growth has in fact slowed much more than the headline numbers show (Chart 3.7). For example, the headline export growth rate slowed to 17% in 2008 from 26% in 2007. But the RMB rose 6% against the USD in 2008 from 2007. Hence, adjusting for the RMB appreciation, China's export growth was only 11% (=17%–6%) in 2008. Damages from net exports are certainly a drag on GDP growth, as net exports have risen to 8% of GDP from less than 2% in 2000.

The diversification illusion

Despite China's diversification of export destinations, the US, European and Japanese markets still account for half of China's total exports. Crucially, export diversification has been inflated because many Chinese exports to Asia are re-exported to the developed markets. Hong Kong is an extreme example, with over 80% of Chinese exports to the territory being re-exported to third markets in the USA, Europe and Japan. Adjusting for Chinese re-exports through Hong Kong pushes up the share of Chinese exports to the developed markets by an estimated 11 percentage points (Chart 3.8).

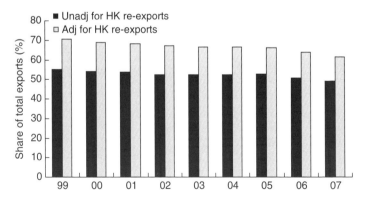

Chart 3.8   Chinese exports to the USA, Europe and Japan
Source: CEIC.

Hence, the USA, Europe and Japan still absorb 62% of China's exports. The reason why China cannot shake off the influence of these developed markets is simple: they are the world's largest consumers, accounting for over 70% of global private consumption, and China has become the world's supplier of consumer goods.

The domestic impact of trade

China's export growth has played a crucial role in absorbing its manufacturing excess capacity. From a different angle, robust export growth has propelled massive capacity expansion in recent years (Chart 3.9). Investment by the export-oriented manufacturing sector has outpaced the total urban investment growth by a wide margin since 2004, with the former rising by an annual average of 35% versus the latter's 26%. The share of manufacturing investment has also jumped to 31% of the total from only 12% in 2002.

There is also a second round effect of exports on domestic investment and job growth which conventional analysis often overlooks. Some analysts argued that, to assess the economic impact of exports, we should examine their value-added by stripping out the trade flow of processing exports. This is because the import components in the processing export trade do not contribute to economic growth. So they should be stripped out to calculate the net export revenue actually accrued to the domestic economy.

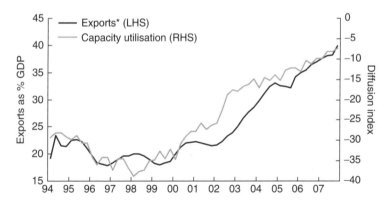

Chart 3.9 Exports absorbing capacity utilisation

Note: * 4-qtr moving average.

Source: CEIC.

However, processing exports do affect domestic investment and job growth via investment in assembling plants, machinery and logistic services and hiring of local labour to assemble the imported inputs into end products before exporting them. An expansion in processing exports has also been an effective channel for technological upgrading, a key engine for productivity growth. Thus, cutting them out will lead to underestimation of the economic impact of exports on the domestic economy.

Rapid expansion in manufacturing capacity has also created spillover demand for energy, freight and transportation, and trade-related services, boosting investment in power generation, coal mining, highways, railways, ports and real estate in industrial parks. These areas combined account for at least another 20% of total urban investment. This means that the manufacturing sector drives over half of total urban investment (Table 3.2).

On the job front, the manufacturing sector hires over 120 million workers, or about 40% of the total urban employment. However, among the rest of the 60% of jobs in the tertiary sector, almost two-thirds are casual, low-paid, temporary jobs. This means that the manufacturing sector's share of total formal jobs is quite significant. Obviously, formal jobs are more secure and deliver better income growth than low-paid informal jobs.

Table 3.2   Urban fixed-asset investment breakdown (2007)

	% of total
Manufacturing	31
Real Estate	24
Infrastructure	29
Power, water and gas supply	8
Transport and telecom	11
Urban infrastructure	10
Others	16

Notes: * Assuming 40% of real estate and infrastructure investments are manufacturing-driven ⇒ 21.2% of these are related to manufacturing; adding this to manufacturing's 31% share ⇒ a total of 52.2% of urban investment is manufacturing-driven.

Source: CEIC.

The economic bottom lines

China's integration into the global economy implies that the links between global demand and Chinese domestic investment and job growth are much tighter than before. Despite export diversification, the USA, Europe and Japan are still the key markets for Chinese exports. A significant slowdown in their growth as a result of the subprime crisis will have a bigger-than-expected impact on slowing China's growth.

The export sector will be hit hard for many years, especially the low value-added labour-intensive segment, including toys, white goods, textiles and shoes, because the post-subprime-crisis economic adjustment will last for a long time (see Chapters 2 and 9). Many small and medium-sized Chinese exporters will fail in this external shock. Thus, service providers (banks, transport, IT, logistics and property) and cities/provinces with large exposure to these economic victims will see rising risk to their operating environment.

Banks with major exposure to small and medium-sized exporters will likely see deteriorating asset quality and rising bad debts. Throughput growth in some ports, notably those in Guangdong and Fujian, and traffic flows in some coastal provinces, notably in Guangdong, Zhejiang and Jiangsu, will slow sharply because they all have high export/GDP ratios and focus on low-end export products.

Even some regional property markets within China will be hurt, notably in Guangdong, whose export/GDP ratio is over 90%. A significant slowdown in exports will result in not only plant closures and worker layoffs but also layoffs/relocation of company executives. This will cut demand for commercial, industrial and residential properties. In fact, Dongguan (Guangdong's most dynamic export base) became the first major Chinese city to see falling property prices when the subprime crisis deepened in 2008. As real demand falls, speculative demand for properties will disappear quickly, adding to the downward pressure on property prices.

The debt–deflation risk

Some also worry that China will fall into a debt–deflation spiral (TWN, 2009), which would hurt its long-term growth and asset values in the coming years. Such a worry is not unfounded, but it should not be exaggerated. Deflation, or price declines, resulting from productivity gains, falling energy prices and other positive supply shocks may boost consumer spending without much hurting corporate sector margins. This is good deflation. But if deflation results from negative demand shocks, like the current subprime crisis, it is destructive. Crucially, if deflation is mixed with a heavy debt burden, it becomes deadly for the economy. That is because, when debt-laden firms and households rush to repay loans as credit dries up, such behaviour hurts demand and leads to more price cuts. This, in turn, raises the real debt burden, prompting more de-leveraging and creating a vicious debt–deflation spiral.

The risk of debt–deflation in China cannot be ruled out. In fact, in the late 1990s the economy showed some signs of a deflationary spiral that destroyed corporate profits, raised bad debt levels and partly contributed to the sharp contraction of the state-owned enterprises (SOE) sector. However, a debt–deflation scenario is unlikely this time around. First, China's corporate sector has gone through a major de-leveraging process so that overall debt burden has been falling since the late 1990s (Chart 3.10). This reduces the risk of debt–deflation. Second, the debt burden in the household sector is very small, with total consumer loans (mortgage and other personal

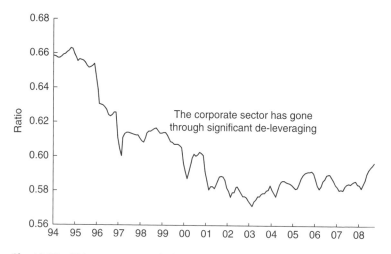

Chart 3.10   Chinese corporate liability/asset ratio*
Note: * 3-mth moving average.
Source: CEIC.

loans) accounting for about 12% of GDP and household deposits accounting for a whopping 70%. This implies a conservative consumer balance sheet, and that does not constitute any pressure for forced de-leveraging in the household sector.

Further, health of the banking system has improved, with a low bad debt ratio of about 7%, down sharply from over 25% in the beginning of this decade. Liquidity in the system has also been rising, as reflected by the decline in loan-to-deposit ratio to 65% from almost 90% a few years ago (Chart 3.11). All this means that the Chinese banks are not under acute pressure to call in loans and, thus, will not force borrowers to de-leverage by dumping assets in the market. This will help prevent deflationary pressures from intensifying.

Hence, the structure of the economy suggests that the odds of debt–deflation emerging in China in the post-subprime world would be very low. There were even some signs in late 2008 and early 2009 that the economy might have been responding to Beijing's stimulus measures. In both December 2008 and January 2009 money and lending growth numbers showed very strong rebound. Steel output also jumped sharply at the end of 2008, with steel prices up by over 10% across most product categories. Last but not least, the Purchasing Manager Index (PMI) improved for three months in a row from

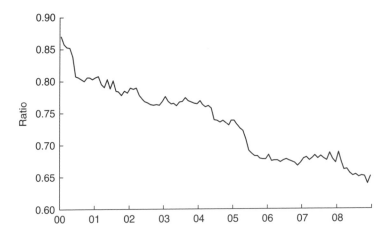

Chart 3.11   Falling loan-to-deposit ratio
Source: CEIC.

December 2008 through February 2009, suggesting a lessening of contraction pressure in the manufacturing sector. It is likely, according to my forecast, that the stimulative impact of Beijing's policy easing will become clearer as this book goes into print, and China will likely become the first major economy to recover from the financial tsunami.

4
Macroeconomic Implications and China

Before the subprime crisis, there was hype among western analysts about China decoupling from the economic growth trend of the developed world. Many investment bank economists were pushing the idea of China becoming an independent economic power that could grow organically and at the same time propel global economic growth. In the early stage of the subprime crisis, many people even thought that China could replace the USA as the world growth driver and save the global economy from imploding under the global credit crisis. These thoughts are naïve. Globalisation and China's internal growth imbalances clearly indicate that there had been no decoupling of Chinese growth and that China could not save the world at this stage of economic development. The subprime crisis has, meanwhile, offered valuable lessons for China's economic policies and for understanding long-term risks in the Chinese banking sector.

Implication 1 for the world: no decoupling of China

Chinese exports contracted sharply under the weight of the subprime crisis, with the damages spilling over to the domestic sector (see Chapter 3). So, contrary to conventional wisdom, China was not bucking the global trend of economic slowdown. How did those decoupling theorists get it so wrong? The fundamental problem lies in their obsession with China's headline growth and ignoring its growth structure. Since economic reform started, rural household income has, on average, grown at about 65% the rate of overall GDP growth, but with the growth gap widening in recent years

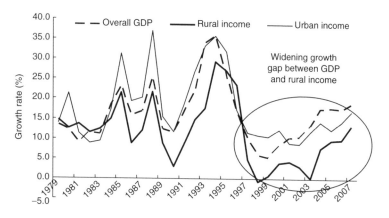

Chart 4.1 Lopsided growth
Source: CEIC.

(Chart 4.1). Urban income has grown more or less in tandem with GDP growth, but the rural population still accounts for the majority (over 55%) of the total population and, hence, the income pool.

The sluggish growth of the bulk of household income combined with rapid growth of GDP means that China has created a huge production capacity at the expense of consumption demand. All this excess output has to go somewhere. And, obviously, it has gone to the USA and other developed markets to cater for their excess consumption (see Chapter 2). Crucially, the persistence of this household income and GDP growth gap suggests that China's growth had been a derivative of US consumption. As US consumption collapsed under the subprime shock, China's growth slowdown became inevitable.

China's lopsided growth problem stems from an imbalance development policy that Beijing has pursued, but is now trying to correct, namely, government-driven supply side expansion. This policy has persistently undermined China's consumption potential, pushing the country to rely on exports to rich countries to absorb the excess production capacity (Huang, 2008). Despite three decades of economic liberalisation, the government's 'visible hand' in driving broad economic direction remains powerful. Beijing still heavily influences fixed-asset investment, which accounts for 45% of GDP and contributes to over half of China's annual growth rate. The government still controls the banking sector, issuing administrative directives for bank lending. Much of the GDP growth since the mid-1990s has been the result of massive government-driven investment drives in infrastructure and urban construction, although 'creative destruction' of the state did take place and contributed to improving GDP growth quality to some extent (Lo 2007).

Implication 2 for the world: China can't save the world

Many foreign investors are impressed with China's business-friendly approach to attracting foreign investment as a way to modernise and industrialise the country. If a foreign firm goes to a local Chinese government and wants to build a factory on some densely populated (or farm) land, the local officials will welcome the proposal with wide open arms and pledge to clear the land within a few weeks. But this 'business-friendly' behaviour is a big problem, because the Chinese households concerned often reap no fair financial benefits from the conversion of their residential (or farm) land into industrial or commercial development.

Since the government owns all the land and there is a lack of effective property rights enforcement framework in China, it can relocate households in a way that a market economy will not do, with compensation far less than the fair market value of the land. Hence, factory owners and commercial operators incur far lower costs in setting up shops in China than in many other, especially developed, countries. From the entrepreneurs' perspective, this practice creates efficiency, since plants and skyscrapers can be erected in about one-third of the time needed in a developed country.

However, from a microeconomic income distribution perspective in a steady state at any given point in time, a cost to one person is an income to another. Developers and entrepreneurs in China incur lower costs, meaning that the income to some other economic agents is also low. And those deriving low income from this modernisation process happen to be the majority of the population, especially the farmers and city dwellers who have little political power to protect themselves. Thus, a mechanism of private wealth creation via urbanisation by small property owners selling out their land to developers at fair market prices is absent in China.

This development policy misstep had not been an issue when the Chinese economy took off from a very low base, so that headline growth benefited most people as a rising tide raises all ships. Now that the subprime crisis has caused long-term damage to China's export-led, investment-driven growth model, Beijing will have to rebalance the Chinese economy by focusing on ways to redistribute income growth and unlock income growth potential rather than being fixated with headline GDP growth. One effective way to achieve this is by setting up a market mechanism for pricing land and transferring land ownership and user rights.

Given all the structural defects in the economy, China's 'law of large numbers', with over 1.3 billion people, a huge land mass, massive US$2 trillion foreign exchange reserves (as at the end of 2008), etc., does not mean that it could save the world during a global crisis. In absolute terms, China is a big economy. But its growth quality is still poor and potential has yet to be maximised. Thus, it only commands a marginal role in the global demand stage rather than being an absolute driver. For example, China consumes about 7.5 million barrels of oil a day, compared with 49.2 million barrels in the developed economies. With global demand falling under the global credit crisis, every 1% drop in the developed world's oil demand will require a 6.6% increase in Chinese oil demand just to offset it. It is clearly unrealistic to expect China to pick up the global slack in the post-bubble economic adjustment period.

It is equally unrealistic to expect Chinese consumption to pick up the American slack and help pull the world economy out the subprime crisis, because the scale of the adjustment is beyond the capacity of China to deliver. For example, a fall in US consumption amounting to 5% of GDP (which is a low estimate, given the scale of damage from the subprime crisis) would require a rise in Chinese consumption amounting to 17% of China's GDP. To achieve this, Chinese consumption growth would have to reach 40% a year: a clear impossibility.

Implication 1 for China: fixing lopsided growth

An obvious lesson from the subprime crisis for China is that it must change its growth model by boosting domestic consumption. The flipside of the US consumer bubble is China's excess saving. Even though Chinese consumption has been growing in recent years, it is still significantly lagging behind the growth of other major sectors

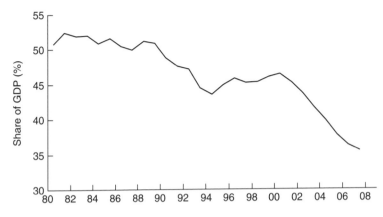

Chart 4.2   China's falling consumption
Source: CEIC.

in the economy. Household consumption only accounts for 36% of GDP, significantly less than the average 60% share in other major economies. Further, China's consumption share of GDP has been declining for years, indicating that the supply-side expansion development model has been eroding domestic consumption potential (Chart 4.2).

The falling share of consumption reflects excessive household saving, which has led to a massive rise in investment spending. The resultant rapid build-up of output capacity has, thus, become dependent on export markets (see Chapters 3 and 9). The combination of rapid productivity growth and a cheap currency policy pursued by Beijing has given the export sector a significant boost, making it a significant driver for investment and economic growth in recent years (Chart 4.3).

The lack of a sufficient social safety net after economic reform took away the freebies provided by the government has been the root cause of China's high propensity to save. While the authorities have recognised this problem, and have taken various steps in recent years to establish more social security coverage and a pension system, the effects have been slow in coming. Sluggish household discretionary spending suggests that the steps taken so far have not been enough. Loopholes in the implementation process are also reducing the effectiveness of the measures.

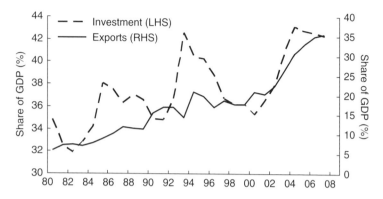

Chart 4.3   Exports driving investment
Source: CEIC.

The damage caused to export growth by the subprime crisis will likely be a multi-year phenomenon because the post-crisis adjustment in the developed world will take a long time, especially if depression-like economic conditions dominate, as some economists have argued (Krugman 2009). This makes the change of China's growth model all the more urgent. The feeble economic environment in the post-subprime-crisis world has given the Chinese authorities a very good opportunity to boost social spending, both as a counter-cyclical policy and as a structural step towards a more balanced growth mix. A bigger domestic sector with higher consumption power is both a necessary and a sufficient condition for China to reduce its economic vulnerability and enhance long-term growth sustainability. More generally, having a clear policy vision is crucial for unleashing China's long-term growth potential, as its growth has come to a turning point where its comparative advantage in labour-intensive production is eroding (Lo 2007).

Implication 2 for China: macro policy directions

China's strong growth in recent years has been driven by an unduly stimulative monetary environment, as seen in a prolonged period of declining real interest rate (Chart 4.4) and an undervalued RMB. The RMB's exchange rate should have risen on the back of strong capital inflows due to a large current account surplus and massive net FDI inflows. But it did not do so until 2005. Even since then,

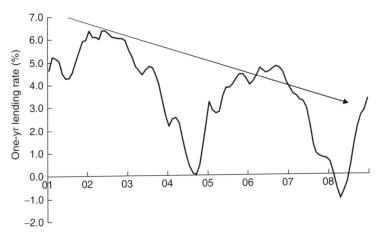

Chart 4.4   Prolonged decline in real interest rate*
Note: * One-year working capital lending rate, 3mma.
Source: CEIC.

the amount of appreciation has not really reflected the underlying upward pressure on the RMB as implied by the balance of payments surplus. Beijing's 'stable currency' policy has barred the RMB from appreciating to the implied fair market levels. Thus, together with a synchronised global economic recovery after the IT bubble in the early 2000s, this environment greatly enhanced Chinese corporate profits, leading to constant pressure on companies to expand.

Beijing recognised the problem in 2004 and started addressing the risk of economic overheating. It adopted numerous restrictive industrial policies and relied mainly on administrative measures, such as lending quota controls, reserve requirement ratio hikes and investment curbs. But all these failed to deal with the fundamental causes of growth imbalance, excess capacity and underconsumption. Further, the emergence of the private sector in recent years has made corporate savings a main funding source for capacity expansion, reducing the effectiveness of Beijing's tightening measures. This, in turn, prompted Beijing to implement more administrative tightening to cool the growth of the targeted sectors in the economy. With hindsight, it can be argued that some of the macro measures imposed between 2004 and 2007 had done little to ease economic volatility.

So, in the post-subprime world, Beijing must establish a proper set of profit incentives and budget constraints to regulate corporate behaviour to prevent future sharp economic swings. More crucially, such incentives and constraints will have to be based on market forces rather than on administrative directives as economic liberalisation deepens. These include the exchange rate, interest rates, bank lending and factor prices such as energy and raw materials. Heavily subsidised electricity prices, for example, were a key driver behind China's massive capacity expansion in the energy-intensive base metals sector, which came under severe contraction pressure amid demand destruction by the subprime crisis.

The Chinese authorities have recently been moving towards liberalising energy prices and other crucial material sectors, but the pace has been slow and needs to speed up in order to achieve any concrete results. The subprime crisis presents a benign opportunity for Beijing to push through some policy breakthroughs. In this regard, the fuel price reform programme that started in 2008 was an encouraging development. The key is to keep the direction and momentum going in the coming years.

Implication 3 for China: Chinese bank risks

The American subprime crisis has reflected both the importance of a functioning banking system and the dire consequences of regulatory failure. Among many other systems, China has also looked to the American financial system and capital markets as a role model for its financial sector reform. As a result, the systemic failure of the American system has sounded an alarm for Chinese regulators. China's hitherto cautious stance towards financial reform has prevented its banks from getting caught in the global credit crisis. But that also means that the Chinese system has remained untested at the time of a modern financial shock.

With China pushing through more financial reforms and developing more financial product markets in the coming years, the US subprime crisis should serve as a valuable lesson for the Chinese authorities to avoid similar policy missteps and growth traps in the future. This is especially crucial as China is considering the development of a credit derivative market and starting to build a consumer credit system. At this moment, personal loans in the form of car,

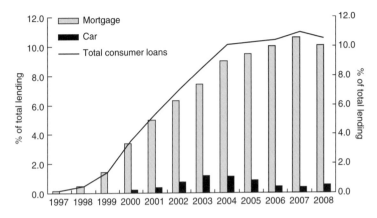

Chart 4.5 Consumer loans remain minimal in China
Source: CEIC.

credit card and mortgage loans in China are very small, accounting for only about 11% of total bank lending (Chart 4.5). Mortgage lending has been very conservative and inflexible. But a more developed financial system and increased access to credit for the consumers are essential for building a consumption-based economy.

There are signs showing that Beijing has recognised that the US banking system failure was a failure of regulation but not a failure of market forces. Despite the prolonged subprime crisis, China still moved ahead with new financial liberalisation rules in 2008. These included allowing margin trading in the local stock market, legalising and regulating part of the informal credit network (or underground financing) among the private enterprises as the first step towards reducing systemic risk and distortion to the credit market, and increasing access to bank credit for small and medium-sized firms. There are other policy initiatives under consideration, such as implementing a futures market, setting up a second-board stock exchange for high-tech start-up companies and relaxing capital controls further. All this suggests that the global credit crisis has not deterred China's resolve to carry out financial reforms. Again, the key is to keep the direction and momentum going in the post-subprime environment. But this may not be easy (see below).

The domestic banking development outlook may be benign. But the story is different from the perspective of the Chinese banks' connection with the rest of the world after the subprime crisis. In late 2008 and early 2009 foreign banks, including Bank of America in the USA, UBS in Switzerland and the Royal Bank of Scotland in the UK, were all trying to cash out in China by selling their strategic stakes in the Chinese banks after the expiry of the three-year lock-up period. They need the cash back home to plug the black hole inflicted by the subprime crisis. The withdrawal of these strategic partners and foreign interests, if continued, will bode ill for China's strategy of using foreign expertise to build a world-class banking system.

Between 2005 and 2008, foreign financial institutions pumped over US$25 billion into Chinese banks as part of the deal engineered by Chinese financial regulators. Foreign investors would gain access to China's banking market and in return transfer management technology to Chinese banks for them to become profitable commercial entities. The momentum for cooperation was slowing even before the subprime crisis due to mismatched expectations and disappointment at what each side had delivered. A common case in point is risk control systems. Chinese bankers are often frustrated by foreign advisors who have rich international knowledge and technical skills but cannot adapt to the local markets and solve local problems. That is altering the Chinese bankers' expectations that foreign advisors will be able to offer effective solutions. On the other hand, foreigners have felt betrayed by their limited influence over bank operations and their inability to gain ownership control. Foreign strategic investors have been expecting a lifting of the 20% cap on foreign stakes in Chinese banks, but that has not happened.

When China opened up its banking sector for strategic investment in 2005, it hoped that foreigners would help improve Chinese management standards, transfer technology and know-how, and co-build new fee-earning businesses such as credit cards and wealth management. Most crucially, China hoped the foreign banking partners would help improve risk governance in the Chinese banking system. But all these hopes will be gone after the foreigners have sold their stakes in the Chinese banks. Meanwhile, after the subprime crisis, the Chinese regulators are also debating what benefits China could get from the western banking model and practices. If both sides turn cool towards Sino-western cooperation, there will be the risk of a slowdown in China's financial liberalisation in the future.

5
Regulatory Lessons from the Rescue Efforts

At the time of writing, bailout efforts by the global authorities to contain the economic damages of the subprime crisis are still ongoing and evolving. But the development hitherto has offered significant insight for discussing some regulatory lessons that can be learned. Only since October 2008 have we seen a big change in the western authorities' policy attitude – from disorganised to concerted efforts – towards handling the subprime crisis. But there have been no collective efforts in Asia, at least not to a similar extent as in the western world, to deal with the crisis, mainly because there is no such need to do so. The Asian response aims at fending off the economic shocks stemming from the western world's financial crisis via trade links. Hence, the response is basically of a macro policy nature and includes liquidity injection, deposit guarantees, and interest rate and bank reserve requirement cuts. The different responses from the different authorities have offered valuable regulatory lessons for dealing with a significant financial shock like the subprime crisis. This crisis is unprecedented, as there have been no similar previous incidents that have caused such a devastating impact on confidence in the global financial system.

The western world's aggressive response

Europe

Among the major crisis areas in the western world, Europe has had the most disorganised rescue approach. The main reason is the lack of one single financial regulator and treasury for Europe. There are twenty-seven member states in the European Union; even in the smaller Euro zone, there are sixteen member states. Different states have different voices, so that there is a lack of coordinated response to the crisis.

This lack of coordination has forced Europe into a case-by-case approach, at least in the early stage of the crisis, in assuring depositors that their financial systems will be protected. This is not only expensive, but also not sustainable. How many Fortises or Dexirs or Hypo Real Estates can one government save? Crucially, this short-term fix saves bad banks at the expense of good ones. Delaying the process of forcing weak banks to close will only slow the normalisation of lending and encourage moral hazard, which could be even more costly to taxpayers down the road.

After the subprime crisis deepened in late 2008, many European countries, including Germany, Denmark, Ireland and Iceland, adopted blanket guarantees on all deposits in their banking systems to prevent further loss of confidence. This was later followed by other countries, including the USA and the UK. However, even at the time of writing (one-and-a-half years after the crisis broke), Europe has remained a troublesome spot in terms of dealing with the subprime crisis. It will remain so until it comes up with a concerted approach to resolve the crisis. The key problem for Europe is that it has too many voices and political interests being forced into the straight-jacket of one macro policy framework.

The USA

The USA started off with a piecemeal bank recapitalisation approach in dealing with the crisis. This did not work, however, because the recapitalisation was triggered by bank failures and, hence, had only dealt with the crisis's symptoms. As the credit crunch pulled down asset prices indiscriminately, what was at first a liquidity crisis soon turned into a solvency crisis for individual banks. The government was then forced to step in and recapitalise the banks, only to find out later that, when another wave of liquidity crisis hit, the capital it injected had evaporated. This vicious cycle just forced the government to throw money into a black hole!

Then Treasury came up with the Troubled Assets Relief Programme (TARP) on 14 October 2008, providing US$700 billion to buy dud mortgage assets from the banks. The TARP aims at creating a floor price for these bad assets so that banks and companies will stop dumping them on the market to create a downward price spiral. While the TARP tries to deal with the banks' solvency problem, it does not deal with the funding issue. It needs to be paired with a scheme for recapitalising the financial institutions so that they can lend again after offloading their dud assets to the TARP.

Alongside the TARP, the US government also temporarily raised deposit insurance from $100,000 to $250,000 to help preserve public confidence in the banks. It promised to follow in the footsteps of Europe and implement a blanket guarantee on all deposits if the confidence crisis continued. In February 2009, the government implemented new measures for restructuring the American banks, using a combination of insurance that would limit bank losses, recapitalisation and a fund buying toxic assets from banks. It also set up a scheme to help reduce foreclosure in order to limit the impact on the consumer. More measures are in the works, at the time of writing, to contain further financial damage to the American banks from spreading. These include the bank 'stress test' to assess how much public funding will be needed to keep America's large banks afloat under a worst-case scenario of a deep and long economic recession.

The UK

The UK authorities had tried to tackle the deficiency in the US approach by addressing both solvency and funding. In late 2008, alongside expanding its liquidity scheme, the UK government injected GBP25 billion of capital into UK banks (with another 25 billion pounds standing by) and guaranteed GBP 250 billion in bank debt for up to three years.

While the UK approach has its appeal, its implementation is more difficult in the USA because the UK banking system is simpler, with eight big, systematically crucial, British financial institutions dominating it. So identifying them for bailout is relatively easy. But the US system is more dispersed, with a greater variety of institutional structures outside the conventional banking sector. That makes the bailout decision more difficult.

In early 2009, the UK government also rolled out measures featuring a kind of insurance that would limit losses on mortgages and other loans. The insurance was aimed at easing worries about the extent of banks' losses so as to revive the market for securities into which banks repackaged the loans. Under the scheme, banks and building societies had to pay 'an insurance premium' to the government for its provision of protection against future defaults on bank loans. The government also put in a guarantee programme for asset-backed securities, which will provide full or partial guarantees to top-rated, triple-A assets.

Bailout approaches converged

Before October 2008, there was no coordination between all the subprime crisis countries. They had only taken ad hoc steps to stem the crisis. Central banks had cut interest rates, governments had acted to strip toxic assets off bank balance sheets and regulators had injected capital into the banking sector. These moves were country-by-country solutions and had no broad coordination between governments, despite the fact that the global financial system was linked. No wonder they had failed to calm the markets and prevent the crisis from deepening.

However, after the demise of Lehman Brothers, AIG and Merrill Lynch in September 2008 took the world financial system deeper into the subprime crisis, the global authorities finally woke up to reality and acted collectively. First came the converted interest rate cut on 8 October, followed by a series of partial nationalisations of the banks and unconventional measures to break the credit deadlock.

The USA had caught up with the concept of expanding funding alongside tackling bank solvency. The Fed decided to bypass the banking system to lend directly to the non-bank corporates by buying commercial papers. It also vowed to keep interest rates low for as long as necessary to revive the credit market, and to buy long-term US government and government agency bonds to keep long-term interest rates low. These moves were more crucial than the TARP to break the credit logjam in the system. They allowed companies to obtain funding which the banks were reluctant to provide. The bond purchase initiative, if implemented effectively, should help keep long-term interest rates low in order to rebuild economic confidence and lower the cost of funding across the economy. But the Fed could not take over all bank lending operations.

So a drastic step is to nationalise the banks temporarily so that the government, as the owner, can order them to lend, thus breaking the credit logjam and reviving credit flows. Europe started such a process promptly as the subprime crisis deepened, and the trend gained traction in both the USA and the UK. Depending on how the crisis evolves, this approach can even be extended to the private debt market, with the government substituting private debt for public debt, or guaranteeing private debt (as the British have done). The temporary nationalisation of the banking system and private debt will allow the financial system to regain a new equilibrium as credit flow restarts, although common shareholders will be wiped out in the process.

Momentum has gathered towards the nationalisation approach among all the crisis countries. This approach is costly and will involve the issuance of more government bonds and higher taxes in the future. But if it can help turn around confidence and revive lending, the cost is worth paying to avoid a global financial implosion and another great economic depression.

The Asian cool response

Asia does not have a financial crisis, despite the global impact of the financial tsunami stemming from the western world. This is mainly because the Asian banking systems, except Korea, have de-leveraged since the aftermath of the 1997/98 Asian crisis. This is in sharp contrast to the over-leveraging of the US and European systems, which sowed the seed for the subprime crisis. This difference in the banking system fundamentals between the east and the west is best summarised by the loan-to-deposit ratio. From a macro perspective, a high ratio (over 100) represents an over-leveraged system, as banks lend more than they take in from deposits; and vice versa. Since the Asian crisis, Asian banks, except Korea, have de-leveraged significantly, while their western counterparts have indulged in lending (Chart 5.1).

Hence, there have not been any coordinated efforts among Asian authorities to deal with the fallout from the subprime crisis because Asia does not have any financial crisis of its own, and it does not have any great exposure to the subprime toxic assets. Further, economic and political diversities among Asian economies have hindered any concerted efforts. But the global credit crunch has raised financial contagion risk and dragged down economic growth in the region. The financial contagion has also pushed up borrowing costs across Asia.

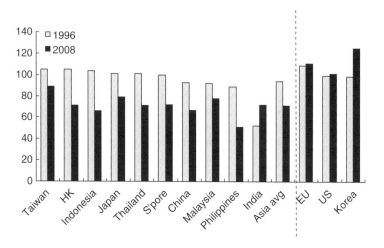

Chart 5.1 Loan-to-deposit ratios
Source: CEIC.

I do not see any big risk of a breakdown in the regional financial transmission mechanism. However, with integrated global financial markets, Asia has seen its stock markets and currencies plunging as risk aversion prompted capital flight from the region. Economic growth across the region has also fallen sharply, especially in small open economies such as Hong Kong and Singapore. Thus, the Asian authorities also had to take action to contain the economic impact of the global credit crisis. The moves basically include liquidity injection, deposit guarantees, and interest rate and bank reserve requirement cuts. Some economies with worse financial imbalances, such as Korea, Indonesia and India, have suffered more from the global financial contagion (see Chapter 9). They have therefore taken more drastic moves to prevent the crisis from spreading, such as guaranteeing local banks' external debt and lending to the local market directly from the treasury.

The following is a comprehensive list of what the major Asian authorities have done in response to the global crisis. New measures are still being considered or implemented as the crisis evolves.

China

Beijing's tactic has been to stabilise and provide support to the economy and asset markets. Up to early 2009, the measures included cancellation of stamp duty on stock purchases, shares repurchase by Chinese banks and easing of property transaction regulations. The People's Bank of China (the central bank) had also shifted to monetary easing by cutting the bank reserve requirement ratio and interest rates. As part of the economic stimulus package, Beijing had also raised and broadened value-added tax rebates for exporters, cut taxes on house purchases and increased fiscal spending to boost investment and consumption. In late 2008, the central government also announced a huge RMB4 trillion (US$586 billion) fiscal stimulus package to boost demand growth, with most of the spending going into infrastructure projects.

Japan

The Bank of Japan (BoJ) did not join in the developed countries' coordinated rate cuts in early October 2008, as its policy rate (at just 0.5%) was already very low, allowing little room for further rate cuts. However, following the steps taken by the Bank of England (BoE), European Central Bank (ECB) and Swiss National Bank (SNB), it lifted the limit on providing dollar funding supply to the local system. The government also expanded deposit insurance, cut individual income tax and granted favourable tax code for corporate capex as a way for the government to inject capital into the financial institutions.

The government had also prepared an emergency package to inject as much as JPY10 trillion (US$100 billion) into the Japanese banks, whose stock prices had been hit hard by the market sell-off. This reflected the seriousness of the global financial contagion, as no one had expected that the Japanese banks would need direct public cash injection. The government had also eased restrictions on banks' shareholding limits, asked the BoJ to buy bank-held stocks, and restarted the Banks Shareholdings Purchase Corp. as part of the stabilisation package. In January 2009, the government agency also instructed state funds to buy Japanese stocks to stem the chronic decline in stock prices and stabilise public confidence.

Korea

Given its domestic credit crisis, Korea had suffered more than other Asian countries from this global credit crunch. To stabilise the banking and financial systems, the government banned short selling of stock and raised the daily ceiling on share repurchases. It also injected US$10 billion into the local won–dollar swap market, supplied US$5 billion to small and medium-sized exporters, bought corporate and bank bonds, guaranteed US$100 billion in newly issued external bank debt, injected liquidity into the local banking system and expanded deposit insurance for principal and interest of insured deposits. The Bank of Korea also adopted a monetary easing stance to help facilitate the economic adjustment process.

Hong Kong and Singapore

Concerns over counterparty risks had resulted in liquidity strains in the banking system in Hong Kong, despite its robust financial backdrop (with an aggregate capital adequacy ratio of the locally incorporated banks at 14%, well above the minimum of 8% prescribed by the BIS). In late 2008, to ease the financial stress, the Hong Kong Monetary Authority (HKMA) injected over HK$5.0 billion into the system, and introduced a more flexible framework for providing liquidity to the banks. The HKMA also cut interest rates and introduced a blanket deposit guarantee to boost depositors' confidence. The Singaporean government had done the same. Furthermore, the Monetary Authority of Singapore had pledged to inject liquidity into the financial system whenever needed and allowed the tightly controlled Singapore dollar trade-weighted index to move down as a means for monetary easing.

India

A current account deficit, a slowdown in capital inflows and a large fiscal deficit had prompted the Reserve Bank of India (RBI) to cut interest rates sharply and increase deposit insurance to boost confidence on the back of the subprime shock. In particular, the RBI injected cash to stop a bank-run on the ICICI Bank, one of the largest banks in India, increased the QFII (qualified financial institutional investors) limit for corporate bonds, accepted all sole bids at bond repurchase auctions, extended the special fixed repo rate to commercial banks to increase liquidity, eased commercial borrowing conditions, and removed the limit on funds raised for rupee expenditure. All these measures were aimed at stemming capital outflow and easing the liquidity constraint in the local system.

Pakistan

The subprime crisis had caused significant concerns about counter-party solvency and liquidity hoarding. In response to continuing tight interbank lending conditions, the State Bank of Pakistan (SBP) cut the bank reserve requirement ratio sharply to pump liquidity. Crucially, through the imposition of the advances-to-deposits ratio, starting in November 2008, banks must cap their advances at 70% of deposits. The SBP is effectively forcing banks to rely primarily on deposits to fund their lending rather than on interbank or whole-sale funds. The move is meant to reduce the risk/impact of a seizure in the credit market. The subprime-induced turmoil in financial markets around the world also showed that deposit funding, when combined with robust deposit insurance or government guaran-tees, was a more stable funding source than interbank or wholesale funding.

Rest of Asia

Following the coordinated interest rate cuts by the major central banks in October 2008, Taiwan and Vietnam also cut interest rates sharply. And to ease the funding needs of liquidity-strapped financial institutions, Indonesia, Malaysia, the Philippines, Taiwan, Thailand and Vietnam had moved to guarantee all bank deposits.

To stabilise the stock market, Indonesia shut it down on 9 and 10 October (a move not recommended by free market principles). The government also temporarily removed the daily limit of share buyback volume and allowed share buyback without shareholders' approval. From November 2008 onwards, banks have been allowed to use performing loans as collateral for short-term financing assist-ance from the central bank. The government also extended the for-eign exchange swap duration from a maximum of seven days to one month so as to give banks and market participants more room to adjust their portfolios, and cancelled limits on the daily balance of short-term foreign borrowings.

Taiwan introduced measures for buying stocks in the local stock market by the state-owned National Stabilisation Fund, banned short-selling, and cut stock transaction costs. Meanwhile, Malaysia doubled the size of the state-owned fund Valuecap Sdn. to support stocks. The central banks in Malaysia and the Philippines had also pledged to stand ready to provide liquidity whenever necessary.

Malaysia was guaranteeing interbank obligations of banking institutions, and the Philippines treasury was lending US dollars directly to domestic financial institutions.

Defensive Asia

With the exception of Korea and India, these financial rescue packages should be seen as pre-emptive moves by the Asian countries. While the western world's key policy objective is to break the credit logjam and revive financial confidence, the top priority in Asia is to support growth, because Asia has no crumbling financial systems. The depressed capital market is an additional hurdle for firms wishing to obtain liquidity. However, banks in Asia with low delinquency ratios and high capital ratios should be better able to withstand the credit crunch than weaker ones and those in economies with worse external balances, such as Korea, India and Indonesia.

Overall, from a fundamental perspective, Asia has piled up sufficient savings to finance its investments and keep growth from slumping on the back of a major decline in export growth. The fall in commodity prices should ease headline inflationary pressures and allow Asian policymakers to ease monetary policy to help shore up growth in the post-subprime environment.

Blanket guarantees for depositors will introduce distortions to the banking system by distorting the incentives for prudent risk management by banks and for exercising due diligence by depositors. This will, in turn, cause moral hazard. That is why all the blanket deposit guarantees implemented by the authorities are of a limited lifespan.

The painful lessons

Despite all these micro, macro and unconventional measures taken by the global authorities to tackle the global credit crisis, the root problem has yet to be dealt with effectively. That is because what the western policymakers have done is to sustain household leverage and consumption at any price, when the only exit from the 'credit quake' involved a return to thrift by the overleveraged. Since this cannot be done without pain, there is still a fair amount of denial among the global authorities. As for China, which is moving along the financial deregulation path and moving to boost consumption as its growth driver in the future, there is a lot for the Chinese regulators and economic policymakers to learn from this crisis and western authorities' policy reactions.

This global credit crisis was rooted in the irresponsible social behaviour of the USA and most of the developed world in the past two decades, which prioritised the desire for current consumption over the ability to pay for it. Financial engineering and deregulation had encouraged borrowing and discouraged thrift to finance excess spending via a gigantic credit bubble. That, in turn, led to huge global economic imbalances and distortions. This root cause explains why it is so difficult to solve the crisis. Desperate to preserve the value of asset prices inflated by this huge liquidity bubble, western policymakers have avoided the painful solution of allowing market clearing. The bailout programmes, liquidity injections and fiscal stimulus packages are all meant to sustain asset prices, when these asset prices really need to fall to market levels so that they can be cleared. Delaying this process only prolongs the crisis.

Japan's experience in the 1990s shows clearly that, if the market were not allowed to clear, the financial crisis would just drag on. Although debt-deflation may be avoided, the economic recession will last a long time and the recovery will be weaker. World Bank research shows that accommodating measures, such as massive liquidity support, blanket deposit guarantees, regulatory forbearance, repeated recapitalisation and debtor bailouts (which are all the measures that the global authorities are using in this crisis), appear to raise sharply the costs of banking crises (Klingbiel *et al.*, 2002). There was no evidence from the World Bank study that these accommodating policies could achieve faster economic recovery.

There is nothing mysterious about the right policy to solve the subprime crisis, as is shown by the Scandinavian banking crises in the early 1990s. The banks must be forced to disclose their toxic assets and then these must be written down to market prices. This means that shareholders and bondholders will be hit hard, but depositors should be protected. The Swedish model stands out as a prime example of the success of tackling a financial crisis by adopting the 'good bank bad bank' model.

The Swedish government set up a 'bad bank' in 1992 to buy all the toxic assets from the banking system at market prices, forcing the

Swedish banks to write down these assets and take the hit to their equity before any recapitalisation could begin. This should enable whatever is left of the smaller 'good bank' to be commercially viable again. Even by mid-2009, this has not happened in the subprime crisis countries, including the USA, UK and Europe. However, the ultimate endgame in the crisis countries is likely to be nationalisation of most of the banking system, as the logic of such action becomes overwhelming. Obviously, there are powerful vested interests wanting to prevent such an action of last resort.

Relying on an insurance scheme to limit the banks' losses, as adopted by most of the western authorities in early 2009, does not solve the underlying problem that clogged the credit flow. What the insurance does is to eliminate the banks' risk exposure to the toxic assets, but the toxic assets still remain on the bank books. Unless the toxic assets are taken off the banks' balance sheets, the whole system remains as corrupted as before. The bad assets will continue to suck resources out of the system in the form of zombie borrowers, misallocation and mispricing of capital, public sector debt and budget deficits.

Hitherto, the US government alone has spent a huge amount of money on containing the subprime crisis – enough to fund two Vietnam Wars. About 90% of this money has been spent on sustaining lending and consumption. But this bailout strategy has not attacked the root causes of the crisis – overleveraged asset financed by excessive credit creation. Here is the most relevant lesson for China, which is very much used to the idea of spending its way out of economic problems. It is possible that the sheer size of all these spending programmes may eventually overcome the structural failures of the financial system and produce an economic recovery. But, if such profligate policies do produce economic recovery, they will only do so by creating more and bigger bubbles, with the same final result of collapse at an even grander scale. So it is better for China to heed the lessons now and make a good start on its efforts to deregulate the financial sector and develop a consumer credit market, rather than jumping into financial engineering and excessive consumerism and ending up with another big financial mess to mop up in the future.

6
What Can We Learn from AIG's Collapse?

AIG's failure in the subprime crisis carries significant implications for financial regulators, especially the Chinese regulators, who are deregulating the insurance sector and considering the development of a credit derivatives market in the country. Regulatory loopholes allowed AIG to stray away from its core business; notably into the credit default swaps (CDS) business that triggered its failure. Asset–liability mismatch in AIG's securities lending programme worsened its liquidity problem, turning it into a solvency problem. The moral of the story is that insurance companies must not be tempted to maximise short-term profit; risk control is of paramount importance to avoid an AIG fate.

In considering the development of a CDS market or equivalent business, the Chinese regulators and insurance companies should note that credit risk analysis and assessment are more crucial than return maximisation as a business strategy. Indeed, any insurance company getting into the CDS business needs to be more stringent than usual on risk controls, including macro and policy risks, liquidity risk, credit risk and operation risks. Finally, CDS could become deadly, wreaking havoc in the whole financial system with devastating power, in the case of collusive behaviour by speculators. All this argues for proper regulation of the CDS market.

The failures of AIG, Fortis and Lehman Brothers share a common macro background, namely the bursting of the US housing bubble, which exposed the structural flaws in the developed world's financial systems after more than two decades of deregulation. The benign economic environment behind the US asset bubble bred moral hazard, regulatory oversight and imprudent investment and lending decisions. Securitisation, with the original good intention of risk diversification, backfired under this backdrop and let the subprime problem grow. The diversified risks, bundled in derivative products, complicated the subprime crisis by intensifying contagion when confidence in the global banks collapsed.

However, the micro backdrop for AIG's downfall is different from that of Fortis and Lehman Brothers. Each case has some different lessons to be learnt. We examine the AIG case in this chapter and the Fortis and Lehman cases in the next.

The fall and rescue of AIG

American International Group (AIG) is the largest commercial insurer in the USA. It operates in general insurance, life insurance, financial services and asset management. This world insurance leader had assets of over $1 trillion by the end of June 2008, but became illiquid in mid-September and had to be bailed out by the US Federal Reserve.

The collapse of AIG was not caused by its core insurance business. Rather, its huge exposure – $441 billion (as of June 2008) – to CDS was the trigger. CDS is a swap contract the buyer (usually a bank) buys from an insurance company to insure against default of a credit instrument (in this case collateralised debt obligations, CDO) that it holds in return for payments to the seller (AIG in this case). Out of the $441 billion CDS that AIG underwrote, $58 billion contained subprime mortgage collateral. The mark-to-market losses as of June 2008 were about $25 billion, of which $21 billion were related to the securities containing subprime mortgage collateral. The losses will keep growing as long as the values of the CDOs and, hence, CDS keep falling.

Between 2001 and 2006, when the housing market was booming, all banks wanted to tap into the mortgage market by investing directly or indirectly through mortgage-backed securities (MBS) and CDOs. Due to the new Basel II regulations around the world, the riskier the loans a bank owns, the more capital it must set aside as reserves. To get around this regulatory capital requirement, American and European banks took out insurance, by buying CDS, on these high-yielding securities to guarantee their asset quality.

During the housing boom, default rates and default insurance costs were low and the CDS was very profitable for the banks and AIG. But, when the housing bubble burst, the default rate on the mortgages taken out during the boom years soared. All of a sudden, no-one wanted the MBS and CDOs, which caused the market values of these instruments to plunge. This, in turn, prompted the banks to force the CDS seller, AIG in our case here, to put up more collateral to back the CDS securities that it had underwritten. As the mortgage derivates' values spiralled downwards, AIG had to put up an ever-increasing amount of collateral to cover the potential claims, draining its liquidity.

As AIG incurred losses in its CDS, it started raising capital, and in May 2008 it managed to raise $20 billion to repair the losses. However, the losses kept growing along with plunging housing prices and the values of the MBS and CDOs. Then major credit-rating agencies decided to downgrade AIG on 15 September 2008. This rubbed salt into AIG's wounds by raising its funding cost and prompting it to post more than $13 billion of extra collateral with trading partners. Although AIG had huge assets on its balance sheet, they were illiquid (some of the assets were held at the insurance subsidiaries which were subject to regulatory requirements) and could not solve the liquidity problem.

Finally, in October, the Fed stepped in to rescue the insurance giant by buying $70 billion of CDOs that AIG insured. Under the rescue plan, the banks would keep the collateral they received from AIG while selling the CDOs at market prices to the new investment company that the Fed created. This method effectively made the banks whole in exchange for allowing AIG to cancel the CDS contracts it had written (Chart 6.1).

The cancellation of the CDS contracts would free AIG from additional collateral calls on those swaps. This rescue plan was thus aimed at giving the banks an incentive to sell their CODs to the Fed so that AIG could cancel the CDS. It also helped directly address the troublesome parts of AIG's business by targeting the CDOs. The downward spiral of the values of the CDOs would force AIG to put up more and more collateral each day, draining its liquidity and eventually threatening its solvency.

Bank

1. The banks paid AIG (via credit default swaps, CDS) to protect collateralised debt obligations (CDOs) from default

AIG

2. When the CDO values dropped, AIG posted billions of dollars in collateral to the banks to support promises on future payouts

After Fed's rescue plan

3. The Fed will buy $70 billion in multi-sector CDOs, paying market prices. That effectively will make the banks whole because they keep the collateral they collected

4. AIG will cancel the CDS contracts, and free itself from collateral calls

AIG/Fed Facility

Chart 6.1   Rescuing AIG

Causes of AIG's downfall

AIG's insurance business was healthy. It was the mortgage derivatives that pulled it down. First, CDS are technically a type of insurance contract, but, due to their complex structure, they are not regulated as normal insurance contracts. There is no central reporting mechanism to determine their values. Therefore, AIG did not hold enough capital to cover the potential claims and the insured parties had no guarantee that the insurers were able to honour their obligations.

Second, the complex nature of the CDS complicates the risk assessment for insurers. Due to the increasingly competitive insurance market in the USA, insurance companies have all tried to differentiate themselves against each other and to diversify their earnings. This had prompted AIG not only to stray away from its core insurance business, but also to loosen its risk management process and become less transparent to investors.

Third, asset and liability mismatch in its securities lending programme had intensified AIG's liquidity problem. Under the programme, AIG loaned securities to third parties in exchange for cash collateral. This cash collateral in effect became AIG's liability, since it had to return the cash as and when the third parties stopped rolling over the securities loans. Meanwhile, AIG turned around and invested the cash collateral in higher-risk assets (including MBS) which also had longer maturity than its liabilities (i.e. the securities loans).

When the third parties declined to roll over the loans, AIG had to liquidate its long positions but suffered losses from selling the assets in a falling market. This pushed AIG into a liquidity crunch, as the proceeds from selling the assets were insufficient to cover the cash collateral that had to be returned. Thus, after granting AIG an $85 billion credit facility in September, the Fed had to provide an additional $37.8 billion to rescue the company. Up till November 2008, AIG had used $90.3 billion of the credit line from the Fed. Uncertainty still remains, at the time of writing, over how much more the Fed will need to lend to keep the company afloat.

In conclusion, AIG's failure reflected the loopholes in the US regulatory system, the company's poor risk management controls and the asset–liability mismatch practice in its securities lending programme on the back of a sharply deteriorating macro environment. Arguably, the ultimate responsibility of the company's failure rested on its management mischief and the regulatory loopholes. As Federal Reserve chairman Ben Bernanke pointed out 'angrily' in his testimony before the Senate Budget Committee on 3 March 2009 (for example see *Financial Times*, 2009 and Bloomberg, 2009), AIG operated like a hedge fund exploiting regulatory loopholes:

> 'If there is a single episode in this entire 18 months that has made me more angry, I can't think of one other than AIG'
>
> 'AIG exploited a huge gap in the regulatory system. There was no oversight of the financial products division. This was a hedge fund basically that was attached to a large and stable insurance company.' (Ben Bernanke, testimony before the Senate Budget Committee on 3 March 2009)

Implications for China's insurance industry

The Chinese insurance industry has a young twenty-year history and it is still in the early stage of the development curve. It is beginning to shift from its long-time administrative-led principle to a market-oriented one. Currently, regulations are still stringent and product liberalisation is slow. Therefore, the problems at AIG will not emerge in China's insurance industry in the short term.

But market liberalisation is the broad direction of the future. The Chinese regulators are considering the development of debt insurance companies for protecting the financial system by limiting the potential damages from debt securities defaulting. Some are suggesting that the existing large Chinese insurance companies, including China Life, Ping An Insurance, PICC Property & Casualty and Pacific Insurance, could take on this role, while others are suggesting that specialised agencies should be set up to do the job. Whatever form it may take, the move will be equivalent to developing a credit default swap market in China.

The AIG case shows that as an insurance company's structure and business lines become more complex, and as derivative instruments like CDS are not properly regulated (as, in the US, CDS is not regulated by the state insurance regulators or the National Association of Insurance Commission or the Office of Thrift Supervision, which regulated AIG the holding company), moral hazard and the ensuing problems are doomed to happen. Currently, the Chinese insurance industry is dominated by a few large insurers and competition is not intense. But, as the industry develops, competitive pressures could drive insurers to innovate new products. The AIG experience is a valuable lesson for both regulators and insurance companies.

From an operation perspective, insurance companies must not be tempted to maximise short-term profit. Risk control is of paramount importance to avoid an AIG fate. In developing the CDS or equivalent business, credit risk analysis and assessment are more crucial than return maximisation as a business strategy. In a nutshell, any insurance company getting into the CDS business needs to be more stringent on risk controls, including macro and policy risks, liquidity risk, credit risk and operation risks.

As the AIG experience has shown, if not regulated properly, CDS can be deadly because they are derivative instruments traded in an unregulated, opaque, over-the-counter market, where prices can be easily manipulated. More crucially, CDS could produce unintended devastating effects on the economy if banks use CDS as a dynamic credit pricing tool, but the CDS market is exploited by speculators who collude to maximise profit at the expense of financial stability. This implies that risk control must be thorough across different financial segments – banks and securities in particular – to minimise the unintended fallout of the CDS. This implication is especially crucial for China's financial watchdogs because of their intention to develop a CDS or equivalent business in the country. Financial regulators in the developed world should also rethink the implications of allowing banks to use CDS as a tool for determining loan interest rates.

In 2008, some US banks started tying commercial loan interest rates to the price of a borrower's CDS. The intent was to price loans more accurately according to their underlying risks. A riskier borrower will presumably have a higher CDS price and so the bank will want to charge a higher interest rate to be commensurate with the risk. However, this apparent safeguarding of the loan also allows speculators to bet that a borrower's stock price will fall while ensuring that the bet pays off by manipulating the borrower's CDS price upward. Higher CDS prices raise the borrower's interest expense and impair its earnings capability. Falling earnings, in turn, cause the borrower's stock price to drop, allowing the speculators to make money on their bet on such an outcome. How exactly would this work? Consider this hypothetical situation.

123 is a financially sound company listed on the stock exchange, with active trading volume throughout the year. Like most companies, 123 borrows money from a bank for operations. Out of risk aversion, the bank wants to protect itself against undue credit risk stemming from a rise in economic uncertainty. So it enters a CDS contract with an insurance company to insure against default of 123. It then ties its lending interest rates to the price of 123's CDS.

Now assume three speculators, X, Y, Z, who happen to pick 123 as a target and bet on its stock price falling. So they employ a two-pronged approach to maximise the potential profit from this bet by short-selling 123's stock and by buying put options on 123. Let us also assume that these trades went through without attracting the regulators' attention. Then the speculators start a series of trading in 123's CDS to engineer a sharp fall in the company's stock price.

The speculators' collusive behaviour is crucial here to make a big profit from their bet (Chart 6.2). Speculator X sells 123's CDS to speculator Y at an artificially inflated price; this will not attract

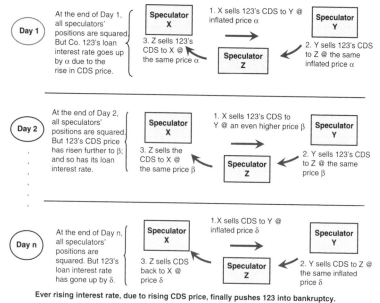

Ever rising interest rate, due to rising CDS price, finally pushes 123 into bankruptcy.

Chart 6.2   Collusion to manipulate CDS price

the regulator's intervention because the CDS market is not regulated. Speculator Y hedges its position by selling the CDS to speculator Z at the same inflated price. And speculator Z hedges its position by selling the CDS back to speculator X at the same inflated price (which also acts as a hedge for speculator X's original trade). So, at the end of the day, all three speculators' positions are squared. The next day, X, Y, and Z engage in the similar chain trading strategy at a higher CDS price; and the next day they do the same at an even higher price. The process could go on for a period of time.

123's rising CDS price raises its interest expenses, as the bank loan interest rate is tied to the CDS price. This, in turn, hurts 123's earnings. Without knowing the speculators' manipulation behind 123's CDS price, equity investors punish 123's stock price when they see its earnings drop. As 123's price falls, the speculators profit from their short-sell positions and put options. But this is not yet the end of the story.

Since 123's interest cost went up, its debt servicing ability went down, pushing its liquidity position into difficulty. 123's creditworthiness worsened sharply due to the speculators' collusion to push up its CDS price and the bank's risk aversion to tie its loan interest rate to the CDS price. Legitimate investors start to trade 123's CDS at higher prices. This hurts 123's earnings, cash flow and stock price further. More speculators join in pushing 123's CDS price higher, creating a vicious spiral of higher CDS price, deteriorating creditworthiness of 123 and higher interest expense. The company tries to stop this death cycle by raising equity and de-leveraging. But its stock price goes into free fall. No-one wants 123's stock, so new equity cannot be raised. 123 finally fails.

This is an unintended consequence of using CDS for dynamic credit pricing according to the change in the borrower's risk profile. Unfortunately, the good intention of financial engineering can be ruined by speculators' self-interest in exploiting regulatory loopholes. The moral of the story is especially important for China's intention to develop credit derivatives, including CDS, and to push for more financial liberalisation in the insurance industry. Financial regulators must keep these financial instruments away from the speculators. Guidelines and safeguards must be set up to control banks tying loan interest rates to CDS prices. Some even advocate an outright ban on banks' dynamic credit pricing by using CDS. Ultimately, credit derivatives like CDS should be regulated properly. The danger of CDS only underscores the developing trend that, in the western world, scope for banks to use, issue, trade and invest in financial derivatives will be limited by re-regulation in the coming years.

7

Different Lessons from
Lehman Brothers and Fortis

Over two decades of financial deregulation and rising competition have prompted financial institutions in the developed world, such as Lehman Brothers in the US and Fortis in Belgium, to develop structured products that are opaque and lack proper risk and regulatory controls. This sowed the seed for a financial disaster. Unlike AIG, the failures of Lehman Brothers and Fortis were more macro-driven, with the bursting of the US housing bubble putting the final nail in their coffins. The developed world banking sector will go through a period of re-regulation. Conventional banking practices will return, while complex financial engineering will be reduced sharply in the coming years of debt liquidation process. The pricing power of the universal banks will grow, due to their dominance in the financial community. This bodes well for the Chinese banking/financial conglomerate model when it comes to overseas expansion.

Collapse of the giants

The collapse of AIG, Lehman Brothers and Fortis shares the same common macro threads of the bursting of the US housing bubble, which exposed the structural flaws of over two decades of financial deregulation in the western world. The similarity stops here. Lehman's and Fortis's downfall had different micro dynamics from AIG's (see Chapter 6). A combination of financial liberalisation, rising competition and imperfect risk management had allowed financial institutions, like Lehman and Fortis, to reap record profits in the past decade through leverage, off-balance sheet investments, securitisation and over-the-counter trading of credit derivatives.

The 158-year-old Lehman Brothers survived the railroad bankruptcies in the 1800s, the Great Depression in the 1930s and the collapse of Long Term Capital Management in 1998, but it failed this time. Lehman filed for Chapter 11 bankruptcy protection on 15 September 2008, thus marking the largest bankruptcy in US history. Barclays eventually bought Lehman's investment banking and trading divisions in North America, and Nomura acquired its investment banking and equities businesses in Asia, Europe and the Middle East.

Fortis was formed in the 1990s through a merger of AMEV, a Dutch insurance company, AG Group, a Belgian insurer, and VSB, a Dutch bank. It was forced into rescue by the Benelux (Belgium, Netherlands and Luxemburg) governments at the end of September 2008. Later, BNP Paribas proposed to acquire part of Fortis's retail banking in Belgium and Luxemburg and its asset management unit, private banking and merchant banking outside the Netherlands. The Benelux governments still retain parts of the Fortis business. At the time of writing, some Fortis shareholders are still fighting to block the BNP deal in the hope that some alternative arrangements may reduce their haircut.

De-regulation and rising competition – a lethal combination

The western world's financial de-regulation started in the 1970s, when then US President Ronald Reagan and English Prime Minister Margaret Thatcher believed that freer markets would bring big economic gains. Following this, the liberalised markets made it easier for homebuyers to get mortgages as credit controls were scrapped, allowing more lenders to enter the home-loan market. Securitisation was also started in the 1970s, with the good intention of diversifying risks so that banks could be made safer. The first big securitisation market was for American mortgages.

Then came the liberalisation of the US securities industry, which dramatically increased competition in the financial sector. The 1933 Glass–Steagall Act, which separated the commercial banking business from securities houses in America, was abolished in 1999. Investment banks and depository institutions were then allowed to compete with each other across the entire business spectrum. Investment banks leapt into commercial banking without the deposit base, while commercial banks went into investment banking without much risk management experience.

The impact spread to Europe. European universal banks, such as UBS, Credit Suisse and Deutsche Bank, limited by the opportunities in their home markets, exploited the US financial liberalisation and expanded their businesses in the USA. They competed with investment banks by taking bigger trading risks, devising off-balance-sheet financing vehicles for securitised assets and setting up new hedge funds.

In recent years, due to competition for deals from cash-rich commercial banks, Wall Street investment banks have found themselves under pressure to provide clients with financing as well as advice. Commercial banks have huge balance sheets backed by cheap retail deposits to make loans. But investment banks have to raise funds, which are typically short-term, in the capital markets as they do not have access to a stable supply of deposit funding. They have also ventured into private equity, putting a growing proportion of their capital into long-term, illiquid investments, such as properties and/ or companies.

This borrow-short invest-long behaviour creates the same balance sheet mismatch problem for the investment banks as for the commercial banks, exposing them to interest rate risk and market volatility. In addition, private equity and hedge funds also compete in the markets for deals and funding. All this has created an immense pressure for players in the financial industry in the western world to explore new sources of profits. This, in turn, has driven financial engineering and increased the supply of exotic financial products.

The increase in supply of financial derivative products was met by rising demand, as investors were also seeking higher-return investment alternatives to fixed income instruments, especially in the period of low interest rates between 2001 and 2006. They bought tranches of collateralised debt obligations (CDOs) or, in the case of leveraged lending, collateralised loan obligations (CLOs), and provided liquidity to these markets. The assets appeared more attractive than they actually were because of the low implied volatilities in the bull market and strong demand. Bankers were more willing to take on bigger credit risks than before because they could securitise the loans and sell them off rather than keeping them on their balance sheets. During the heyday before the crisis, structured finance was a huge income earner, accounting for 30% of big investment banks' profits.

Furthermore, capital is allocated according to the riskiness of assets under Basel II guidelines, which require banks to put up more capital if they hold more risky assets. This has, in turn, prompted banks to make more use of credit derivatives, especially credit default swaps (CDS, see Chapter 6 for definition), to diversify and insure their credit portfolios, in order to get round the capital requirements under Basel II.

Imperfect risk management

The essence of the investment banking business has always been about trading and managing calculated risks. Although investment banks have fewer loans than commercial banks on their balance sheets, they carry more complex exposure, such as collateralised lending to hedge funds. Investment bankers have exploited the business possibilities created by structured products and offered almost limitless ways for their clients to trade and manage risks. Traders have used more complicated ways to speculate clients' money (which we call OPM, or other people's money) in many more different places and markets than ever before. But the problem is that there are no good ways to measure the new risks created by the financial innovation in the past decade.

Hence, risk diversification has backfired. Given the complexity of the new financial instruments and the new range of market participants and countries involved, risk diversification has actually made risk management more difficult because no one knows where the risks actually lie and how to measure and control them. Though risk is diversified more widely, it has not disappeared. Under such circumstances, risk exposures may surface in ways that are hard to predict, especially when so many banks in different countries are exposed to an interlocking web of counterparties.

Things were fine during a bull market, or normal market conditions. However, when the US housing bubble burst (due to the US Fed policy tightening between late 2005 and early 2007; see Chapter 1), the whole benign macro environment underpinning leverage, securitisation and off-balance sheet investment collapsed, pulling the highly geared financial institutions with it.

Lehman's final chapter

According to Lehman Brothers' preliminary third quarter 2008 earnings results, it had $600 billion of asset and only $28.4 billion of equity on its balance sheet. In other words, its leverage ratio was 21.1 times. Lehman was once the biggest underwriter of mortgage-backed securities. The company rode the real estate boom to its peak in the second quarter of 2007, financing property acquisitions and packaging these loans into securities, which it then sold to other institutions. However, Lehman found it hard to find buyers for such securities after two Bear Stearns hedge funds that invested in real estate debt instruments collapsed in July 2007.

With house prices falling, credit deterioration spreading and derivative markets unsettled, Lehman had more than $60 billion of hard-to-sell securities on its book. The bank reported its first quarterly loss in Jun 2008 and wrote off about $2 billion asset. Lehman did come up with a number of strategic moves: spinning off up to $30 billion of commercial real estate assets into a separate public entity (REI Global), and selling a majority stake in its prized fund-management unit. But there were no buyers due to the severe market stress after JP Morgan Chase bought Bear Stearns. There was also uncertainty over the value of Lehman's exposure to illiquid securities. Finally, Lehman had $53 billion of mortgage assets and leveraged loans on its balance sheet, and these toxic assets were almost double the bank's shareholders' funds. As a result of all these, the bank's funding cost soared, cutting off its liquidity.

By the second week in September 2008, Lehman's biggest efforts to appease investors failed. Various Asian and Middle Eastern investors, such as Abu Dhabi Investment Authority and Korea Development Bank, retreated because of the bank's plunging share price and worsening financial strength. Rubbing salt into its wounds, the credit ratings agencies threatened to downgrade Lehman's credit rating unless it found a buyer. A credit downgrade would force the bank to post additional collateral, increase its short-term and long-term funding costs, and limit its ability to transact with partners. The bank made a final effort to sell itself to Barclays and Bank of America. But the bidders asked for risk protection that the Fed was not willing to offer. The bank was left with no choice but to file for bankruptcy protection on 15 September 2008.

Fortis forced into rescue

Fortis might have made the wrong decision on overpaying the ABN AMRO purchase at the wrong time! The €72 billion takeover of ABN AMRO, which was paid for mostly in cash, was the main factor that stretched Fortis's balance sheet. Further, the bank had a sizeable credit spread and structured investment portfolio (around €41.7 billion), which depleted its core equity ratio when these asset values dropped sharply during the subprime crisis.

Despite the €13.4 billion rights issuance in 2007, the €1.5 billion of equity issuance in June 2008, the €1.3 billion saving from deferred dividends and €8 billion in capital raising plans, investors were still concerned about Fortis's ability to raise sufficient capital to absorb ABN AMRO and achieve its 6% core equity target by end 2009. First, Fortis had to pay €24 billion for €4.6 billion of ABN's net assets (which meant effectively €19.4 billion of goodwill and intangibles) that had to be absorbed by the core equity base when ABN was consolidated. Second, impairment on assets, such as the €2.9 billion taken against subprime CDOs and the €41.7 billion credit spread and structure credit portfolios write-downs, hit Fortis's capital base severely. There were other capital demands stemming from forced-selling of assets below book value and other purchase plans, such as the €500 million purchase of Delta Lloyd JV.

Fortis had other critical capital ratios to keep. On the insurance side, it had a target solvency ratio of 175% of equity (a regulatory minimum capital requirement). At the group level, it had a target core equity leverage ratio of 15% of assets, which was a combined core equity target of the bank and insurance subsidiaries. Fortis were running above these targets before the government rescue. But the poor market conditions had prevented it from issuing more equities and selling profitable assets to beef up its capital base. Fortis also had to pay more for raising funds, since borrowing costs soared after the collapse of Lehman Brothers.

Fortis's over-leveraged position only aggravated its dire situation under the global credit crunch. All hopes of staying afloat disappeared when credit rating agencies cut Fortis's long-term credit ratings. At the end of September 2008, Fortis was forced into rescue by the Benelux governments, which injected €11.2 billion into it and took minority stakes in its banking units in each country.

Implications for China

Lehman Brothers' failure may have proven that the stand-alone broker–dealer model is unworkable. The last two major US investment banks, Goldman Sachs and Morgan Stanley, finally converted themselves to bank holding companies in November 2008. Universal banks, such as JP Morgan and Bank of America, may be a better model in the post-crisis environment, due to their diversified income streams and strong retail depository franchises. This means that the developed world banks are going backward, from a de-regulated world to a re-regulated world.

However, the Chinese banks are moving forward towards a more liberal world. In China, banks and some financial institutions, such as Ping An Insurance Group, are pursuing this universal bank model. From a macro perspective, a key lesson from the subprime crisis is that financial liberalisation must go hand in hand with prudent regulations to prevent basic problems, such as over-leveraging, which pulled down Lehman, Fortis and many other western banks, from taking hold. Prudent regulation, but not over-regulation, is far more important for ensuring financial system stability than indiscriminate de-regulation.

Re-regulation of the developed world banking sector is inevitable in the coming years. It implies that the conventional banking model will return. Banks will rely more on stable deposits for funding, and the money markets will become smaller and more expensive in terms of cost of funding. Complex, sophisticated financial engineering practice will be gone for a while, in my view, though some academics and financial engineering professionals disagree, believing that the derivatives market will come back more inventive than ever after the crisis. Finally, in the post-crisis period, the pricing power of the universal banks will likely grow, due to their dominance in the financial community. This bodes well for the Chinese banking/financial conglomerate model when it comes to overseas expansion.

Watch out for 'destructive creation'

On a macroeconomic perspective, one can be optimistic about the handling of this subprime crisis. But, structurally, the root problem of this global 'credit quake' remains not fully understood. In particular, the world has assumed symmetrical outcomes for both non-financial and financial innovation. But in reality the outcomes are not symmetrical. Non-financial innovation leads to creative destruction (for example, see Aghion and Howitt, 1992), which is a positive shock to the economy. But financial innovation leads to 'destructive creation', which is a negative shock.

To see this, let us go back a little to the causes of the US subprime crisis. They were rooted in lending to un-creditworthy mortgage borrowers backed by government agencies Freddie Mac and Fannie Mae. But the problem grew out of hand when financial innovation, for instance the securitisation of mortgages, backfired and created moral hazard, incentive problems and excessive risk-taking. Credit default swaps allowed AIG to reap huge returns, but at high risk if things went wrong; and things did go wrong in the end. Even back in 1998, the Long Term Capital Management crisis had a similar root problem. At its heart were financial derivatives that no one really understood. The same problem of financial innovation backfiring also infected Asia, but in a different form. Arguably, the 1997/98 Asian financial crisis resulted from a macro-financial-innovation failure – namely, the introduction of capital account convertibility in economies that had no proper financial safeguards to control moral hazard and incentive problems. Excess investment thus emerged in the blind faith that the trade-driven robust GDP growth, pegged exchange rate regimes and foreign capital inflows would last forever. The eruption of the regional crisis took the world by surprise and produced an unexpected devastating impact!

In each of these crisis cases, investors and governments made an *ex ante* assumption that both financial and non-financial innovations were the same benign events. But they were not. When the personal computer was invented, the typewriter and even the calculator became obsolete. Their extinction led to other investment and job opportunities, underscoring the benefits of Joseph Schumpeter's creative destruction (Schumpeter, 1975). In the Schumpeter paradigm, non-financial innovation creates an upside for economic growth by destroying the old industries. But, in the modern deregulated world, financial innovation can become devastatingly deadly without creating new growth opportunities. This is the process of what Professor Jagdish Bhagwati of Columbia University called 'destructive creation' (Bhagwati, 2008 and Calvano, 2007).

According to the Bhagwati view, the failure to realise the dire results when financial innovation backfires is rooted in the influence of Wall Street thinking in the US macro policy. Two of the US Treasury Secretaries, Robert Rubin and Henry Paulson, who influenced financial policies for almost two decades, came from big Wall Street firm Goldman Sachs. This Wall Street connection creates the same benign thinking about financial innovation in the US Treasury as in the investment banking circle. Mr Rubin was in charge of the Treasury during the 1997/98 Asian crisis. Mr Paulson was one of the key investment banking chiefs who helped persuade the Securities and Exchange Commission to remain lax on reserve requirement regulations for the investment banks so that their balance sheets could keep expanding in a deregulated environment.

The problem with the Wall Street mentality was that greed eventually overwhelmed prudence on the back of regulatory oversight. Financial policy thinking had become so narrowly focused, or overly optimistic, that it failed to realise the potential downside of financial innovation. Now that the US authorities are trying to undo the wrongs they have done over the past twenty years, the subprime crisis certainly serves as a crucial lesson for the Chinese authorities, who are moving towards more financial liberalisation and creating a credit derivatives market.

8
Quantitative Easing: a Subprime Antidote?

To combat the devastating impact of the subprime crisis, the global authorities have used extreme and unconventional policy tools, one of which is quantitative easing (QE). But this policy move has also created much confusion and misunderstanding about its effects on the economy, inflation and financial markets. Some even question the effectiveness of QE to revive the ailing post-subprime economy because Japan used QE in the 1990s but failed to revive its post-bubble economy. Indeed, the Japanese experience holds valuable lessons for both the US and Chinese economies and financial markets in the coming years. Despite all the grim predictions for economic growth in the post-subprime world, both the US and Chinese economies and asset markets will not, in my view, fall into a Japanese-style quagmire.

Let us start with the US situation under QE. Contrary to common perception, when the US Fed started its aggressive QE policy in autumn 2008, it was not printing money as yet. Indeed, QE will not lead to inflation in the short term. QE's medium-term effect on inflation will depend on how fast the Fed withdraws its monetary stimulus when the economy stabilises. On the back of risk aversion and the post-bubble economic adjustment, QE is more positive for the bond market than for the stock market in the short term. But the US Treasury bond market is another bubble, in my view. It will burst once extreme risk aversion returns to normal. Ironically, QE would not necessarily hurt the USD exchange rate. Its potential impact is unclear because it also depends on the monetary policy of other central banks. The USD is a weak currency in the medium term as part of the adjustment of global imbalances. But risk aversion will keep it strong in the short term.

Quantitative easing = monetisation boosting inflation?

The US Fed started aggressive monetary expansion, dubbed 'quantitative easing' (QE), after the collapse of Lehman Brothers and AIG in mid-September 2008. This can be seen in the fact that the Fed's balance sheet, as measured by the ratio of the monetary base plus excess reserve to GDP, soared from US$900 bn (or 6% of GDP, which is about typical) in September 2008 to over US$2.3 trn (or 16% of GDP) in early 2009.

Reflecting this massive liquidity injection was the effective Fed funds rate (0.125% at the time of writing), which had fallen below the policy target rate of 1% between mid-September 2008 and December (Chart 8.1). The policy Fed funds rate was later cut to a range between 0 and 0.25% in the December 2008 FOMC meeting to accommodate market pressure for a lower interest rate. The gap between the effective and policy Fed funds rates was an outcome of the Fed oversupplying the banks with reserves by buying US Treasuries and other assets. In QE, the Fed seeks to target the level of liquidity (or bank reserves at the central bank), not the interest rate.

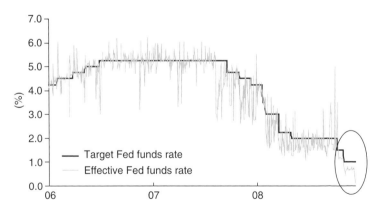

Chart 8.1   The Fed in QE drive
Source: CEIC.

The Fed implements QE in several ways, including various term auction facilities, ad hoc credit lines to specific institutions and direct purchases of commercial papers, government agency debt and asset-back securities. The direct purchase move is meant to bypass the banking system and lend directly to the corporate and housing sectors when the banking sector is unwilling to do so. If these measures fail to revive the credit system, more unconventional measures, including the Fed directly buying long-term US Treasuries, can be expected.

In theory the Fed is printing money, but in practice it is not; at least not in the early stage of QE. Bank reserves at the Fed are part of the base money, or high-power money. Through bank lending, an increase in the base money will lead to a more than proportionate increase in the broad money supply, such as M2. Hence, the ratio of M2 to base money is known as the 'money multiplier', and it relies on bank extending loans to take effect.

However, the problem in this subprime crisis environment (just as in Japan in the 1990s) is that the bank intermediation process has been broken. US banks have scaled back lending sharply by tightening up lending standard (Chart 8.2) and have just sat on their pile of reserves at the Fed. Hence, the money multiplier has collapsed (Chart 8.3), due to the banks' risk-averse behaviour in the subprime

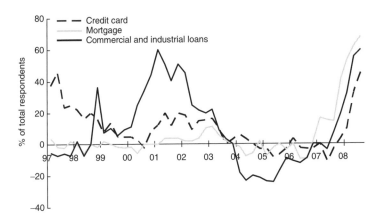

Chart 8.2 US financial institutions tightening lending standards
Source: CEIC.

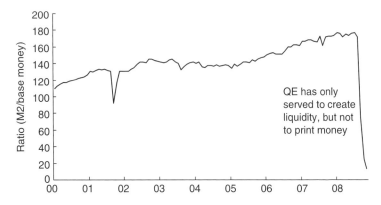

Chart 8.3   US money multiplier has collapsed
Source: CEIC.

crisis. With the money multiplier malfunctioning, the Fed QE has served to create liquidity in the form of bank reserves, but not yet by printing money.

The USA is stuck in a 'liquidity trap', where the banks are flooded with liquidity and the effective funding cost has fallen towards zero, but they are still not willing to lend. The logical solution to this problem is to boost fiscal spending, i.e. to let the government's 'visible hand' pull the economy out of the financial quagmire. Another way is for the Fed to bypass the banking system and lend to the corporates directly.

The huge amount of liquidity pumped into the system via QE will not ignite inflation in the short term. This is because the current liquidity demand is not motivated by the desire to spend, but by the need to offset investment losses and repair confidence in the financial system. This is clearly seen in the sharp decline in money velocity (nominal income divided by M2, Chart 8.4), which is a reflection of the collapse of the money multiplier. In other words, QE in the current situation will only serve to limit the deflationary impact in the coming years, as the economy works its way through a post-bubble debt liquidation adjustment.

In the longer term, the inflationary impact of QE will depend on how fast the Fed withdraws the liquidity when the money multiplier is normalised. It is not difficult for the Fed to end its monetary

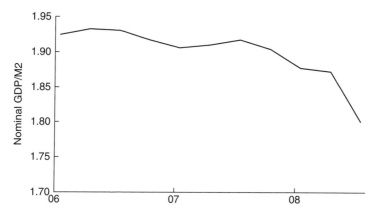

Chart 8.4 Declining money velocity
Source: CEIC.

stimulus through open market operations and sell back the short- and long-term Treasury and other securities that it has bought.

A policy mistake resulting in reignited inflation cannot be ruled out, if the Fed is too slow to reverse QE. But, given the expected long and painful de-leveraging process that the US economy has to go through, QE today does not necessarily point to higher inflation later. Indeed, Japan is a good example. It still has not shaken off the deflationary drag today, despite the Bank of Japan (BoJ)'s implementation of QE for five years between March 2001 and March 2006.

Impact on the USD

QE does not have to hurt the exchange rate by increasing the supply of the currency, because there are other factors at work too. For example, the BoJ implemented QE between March 2001 and March 2006. The JPY/USD exchange rate fell in 2001 only, and then strengthened from 2002 through 2004, when the US Fed cut rates aggressively after the bursting of the IT bubble.

The point is that the impact of QE on the exchange rate (the USD here) also depends on what other central banks do. Against the economic backdrop of the subprime crisis, other major central banks, notably the European Central Bank (ECB) and the Bank of England (BoE), are likely to follow the US Fed's QE path. The European and

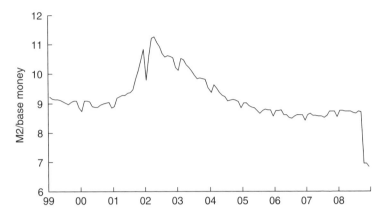

Chart 8.5   Euro zone money multiplier has also collapsed
Source: CEIC.

the UK banking systems have been just as badly hurt by the sub-prime woes as the US system, and their money multipliers are at least as badly damaged (Chart 8.5). The breakdown of financial inter-mediation will eventually force the ECB and BoE down the QE path and act as a financial intermediary on behalf of the private sector.

Further, unless the market expects QE to cause runaway inflation in the USA (which is not my base case), the USD will not collapse. So with no inflation scare, and if the US Fed, ECB and the BoE all adopt QE, there will be no net negative impact on the USD. As long as risk aversion remains high, the USD will remain strong against the major currencies. Over the medium term, however, the USD should weaken, especially against the Asian currencies, as part of the global adjustment process.

The Fed's QE is just plugging the financial black hole caused by the subprime crisis. Financial intermediation is broken, money velocity is falling and the money multiplier is impaired. Inflation will not arise under these circumstances. As long as risk aversion remains high, QE will be more positive for the bond market than for the equity market. The latter will have to climb a wall of worries about earnings growth under debt-deflation in the short term.

The US Treasury market is another bubble waiting to go bust when risk aversion fades. There will be a gigantic number of bonds coming to the market due to the US government bailouts. A sub-3% yield for the long Treasury bond (as has been the case since the deepening of the subprime crisis in October 2008 and after) will be unsustainable when risk-taking behaviour is normalised. Finally, the USD will not weaken under risk aversion and when other major central banks will be forced down the road of QE eventually, though it will probably be a weak currency in the medium term.

Failure of the Japanese QE policy

The failure of Japan's QE policy in the 1990s holds valuable lessons for both the US and Chinese economies and financial markets. Speed of the policy response to the crisis and the policy determination, through the use of unconventional policy tools, to resolve the crisis are key to prevent a Japanese-style prolonged growth recession and deflation. Any policy mistakes that derail the US reflation effort will prolong the economic recession. China has a different problem. It has reacted fast to control the damages from the external shock; and these damages are relatively limited. Its key challenge is to prevent deflation expectations from taking hold. In a nutshell, both the US and Chinese economies and asset markets will not, in my view, fall into a Japanese-style quagmire.

Japan implemented QE between March 2001 and March 2006 in an attempt to save its economy from a post-bubble debt-deflation quagmire. The aim was to flood the domestic banking system with liquidity, reduce long-term interest rates and revive banking lending and credit demand. In its policy statement on 19 March 2001, the BoJ explicitly committed itself to pursuing this policy by announcing that QE would remain in place until non-food-CPI became stable at positive levels.

To pursue QE, the BoJ shifted its target from the overnight policy rate (which was driven down to 0% by the so-called zero-interest-rate policy, or ZIRP) to the level of bank deposits at the central bank (i.e. the BoJ's current account balance). It raised the level of its current account balance to JPY35 trillion during the QE period, well above the JPY1 trillion needed to keep the overnight rate at 0%. Through open market operations, it bought treasury bills and long- and short-term bonds and asset-backed securities. It even bought equities outright to help unwind the cross-holding share structure in the banking system.

But the BoJ's QE efforts failed to boost credit growth and reduce risk aversion as desired. While QE successfully boosted the monetary base, or high power money, its expansionary impact failed to spill over to broad money supply, such as M2. This was because the money multiplier collapsed (Chart 8.6), due to the Japanese banks'

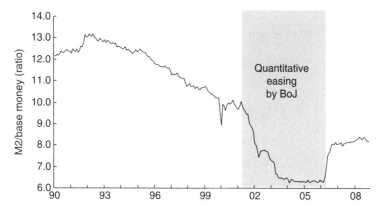

Chart 8.6   Japan's money multiplier collapsed
Note: Shaded area = period of QE.
Source: CEIC.

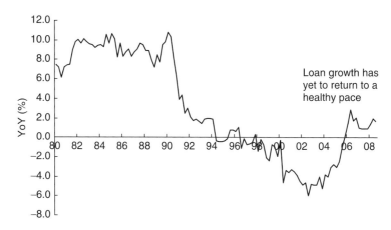

Chart 8.7   Japan bank loan growth
Source: CEIC.

unwillingness to extend loans. The situation was exactly the same as the US subprime crisis. The Japanese banks simply parked their excess reserves at the risk-free BoJ accounts. Japan's bank lending stabilised in 2006, but it has yet to return to a healthy growth rate (Chart 8.7). The only positive outcome of QE was to drive down long-term Japanese Government Bond (JGB) yields to very low levels (1.28% at the time of writing).

What went wrong?

The failure of Japan's QE was a result of a policy mistake; the authorities had kept both monetary and fiscal policies too tight for too long. They were completely insensitive to the debt-deflation environment after the bursting of the asset bubble in 1989. The BoJ even hiked rates by 200 basis points after the stock market bubble burst and kept them elevated for 18 months before it started easing in mid-1991. There was no decisive fiscal expansion for some years, and QE did not start until March 2001, eleven years after the bubble burst.

Massive wealth destruction and weakening aggregate demand had eliminated any underlying inflationary pressures outside the volatile food and energy areas. But the BoJ kept its overly hawkish anti-inflation stance. This created a strong expectation among the public of prolonged deflation, which became self-fulfilling. The BoJ ended QE in March 2006 and started tightening in July 2006, eighteen months before the non-food-CPI inflation rate moved decisively into positive territory (Chart 8.8). By tightening early, the BoJ broke its promise on keeping QE in place to pull the economy out of the deflationary trap!

This policy mistake allowed deflationary forces to take hold and become entrenched, undermining both demand and supply of credit and growth momentum in the economy. The heavily indebted Japanese banks were busy de-leveraging on the back of falling asset values and weakening demand. So they refused to lend. This weakened the economy and asset prices further, causing more deflationary pressures and raising the real debt burden. In response to wealth destruction and job losses, Japanese households spent less and saved more; thus growth suffered further. The BoJ's hawkish stance against inflation only aggravated deflationary expectations, prompting the public to postpone consumption and investment and leading to a vicious debt–deflation cycle.

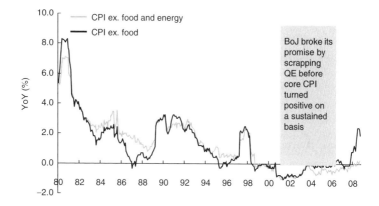

Chart 8.8   Falling inflationary pressures after Japan's asset bubble burst
Note: Shaded area = period of QE.
Source: CEIC.

Lessons for the USA

In the post-bubble world, both Japan and the USA are highly indebted economies suffering from property and other risky asset price declines, which have pushed them into a systemic financial crisis. But the USA is in a less dire state, as its housing bubble is smaller and there is no cross-shareholding structure in the US banking system. What can the USA learn from Japan to avoid a Japanese-style economic quagmire?

First, the reaction to the crisis must be fast and the policy resolve and focus must be strong and clear. Second, the authorities must engage in unconventional policies, such as bypassing the banking system and lending directly to the commercial sectors, recapitalising banks with public money and even nationalising the banks, in order to break the credit logjam. Finally, fiscal expansion must supplement QE to pull the economy out of the 'liquidity trap'.

Hitherto, the US government's reaction to the crisis has been swift, and it has been trying all the policy tools, sending out strong signals that it will do all it can to prevent another Great Depression. From a market perspective, any policy mistakes that derailed the reflation efforts would be very bullish for the bond market, forcing long bond yields down sharply, just like the JGB yields in the 1990s. The Fed's QE policy is bond positive initially, inflating the Treasury bond bubble further before it bursts.

Lessons for China

In some areas, China shows similar symptoms to the USA in this global financial crisis: notably, slowing demand growth and falling asset prices. But the Chinese banking system is not impaired, so its credit market is not damaged; the consumers are not leveraged, so there is no pressure for consumption to contract. The Chinese authorities have also been reacting fast to this external shock. They started easing selectively in August 2008 and turned decisively expansionary in September using monetary, fiscal and administrative tools.

The Japanese experience reveals an important challenge for the Chinese authorities – do not let deflationary expectations take hold. This is because, once entrenched, these expectations will become self-fulfilling and lead to a vicious deflation spiral. China's inflationary expectations started decreasing in late 2008 (Chart 8.9). Core inflation (CPI excluding food and energy) has been stuck at very low levels of less than 2% for a long time (Chart 8.10). On the back of weak consumer and investor confidence, the risk of deflationary expectations becoming entrenched is real.

The People's Bank of China's key challenge in the post-subprime environment is to prevent deflation from taking hold. It has cut interest rates and bank reserve requirements, and engaged in Chinese-style quantitative easing through administrative means, such as scrapping bank lending quotas, increasing bank lending through

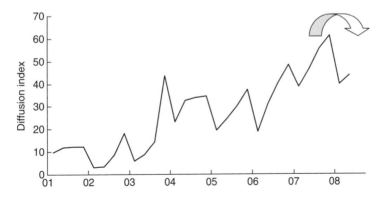

Chart 8.9   Chinese urban residents' future inflation expectations
Source: CEIC.

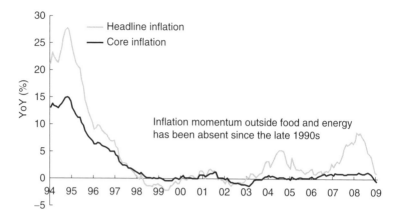

Chart 8.10   China's inherent deflation problem
Source: CEIC.

moral suasion and raising monetary growth targets. Beijing has also complemented the monetary easing by massive fiscal spending. It announced a RMB4 trillion (US$586 million) stimulus package in November 2008 for the next two years to combat the negative economic shock stemming from the external subprime crisis.

In a nutshell, both China and the USA have reacted swiftly to this global financial crisis with all possible policy tools. China also has the advantage of stronger banks and consumers than in the USA. Barring any policy mistakes, neither the Chinese nor the US economies and asset markets will fall into a Japanese-style quagmire.

9
Life After Subprime

The subprime downturn is not a normal economic cycle. We may not see a normal recovery process. Deflationary forces in the post-bubble economy are huge, as debt unwinds across the developed world. There will be periodic goods price and asset price deflation, perpetuated by de-leveraging in the private and financial sectors. Consumption in the developed world will be especially feeble in the coming years. All this will put an end to the emerging markets' export-led development model, crimping profit growth in Asia's export-led economies and sectors. In other words, export-led growth is dead. Asia has not learnt from the 1997/98 Asian crisis experience, so adjustments in both economic and corporate earnings growth terms will be tough this time.

The post-subprime economic adjustment in the developed world will last for a few years, as debt unwinds across all rich countries. In the medium term, global growth will see a structural downward shift, unless developing world consumption rises sharply (but a change in saving habit in the developing world is unlikely in the short term). So governments throughout the world will have to play an active role to prevent their economies from faltering. In the post-bubble world, high-yield investment instruments will be the preferred investment vehicle for as long as the world continues to de-leverage and fight deflation. An infrastructure boom is unfolding in the medium term, favouring commodity and construction-related sectors.

The dark side of the credit boom

Pinpointing the ultimate impact of the post-subprime crisis adjustment on Asia is difficult, due to the complexity of the international credit transmission mechanism. But this impact may be bigger than expected because the great credit boom in the past decade was inflated by financial engineering. Securitisation and the corresponding derivative vehicles had boosted credit demand and supply by an almost limitless amount beyond the traditional balance sheet capacity of lending institutions.

The credit bubble was the financial mirror of excess consumption in many rich economies. Asia's factory economies were the counterparts supplying cheap consumption goods. In the process of catering for this excess consumption, the Asian factories boosted the demand for food and energy produced by other emerging markets. To a large extent, commodity and energy demand had been a derivative of the rich world's excess demand in the past decade.

Excess credit creation in the USA had spilled over to sustain disequilibrium between excess US demand and excess Asian savings. This saving–consumption imbalance had manifested itself in huge US demand for Asian exports and corresponding capital inflows to Asia, resulting in big current and capital account surpluses for Asia. This twin surplus, in turn, fuelled strong growth in Asia via liquidity expansion. But the balance of payments surpluses were so big that Asian central banks (and other commodity-producing economies) recycled a lot of the surpluses back to the USA, keeping US interest rates low and enabling the Americans to generate even more credit expansion.

The coming credit crunch in Asia

Thus, Asia's robust GDP growth rates had been dependent on an unsustainable credit cycle in the rich world. Now the party is over. Savings rates in the rich world will rise in the adjustment process. In the USA, the personal savings rate (as a percentage of disposable household income) has been very low for years. It actually fell below zero in 2006 before recovering a little in 2007 and 2008. This erosion of personal savings was reflected in massive debt build-up. Evidence since 1960 shows the inverse relationship between the savings rate and debt accumulation. From 1960 to 1990, the growth of non-financial debt exceeded nominal GDP growth by 1.5 times on average, while the savings rate averaged 9% a year. From 1991 to 2000, debt growth exceeded GDP growth by 1.8 times, while the savings rate averaged 4.7%. Since 2001, debt has grown twice as fast as nominal GDP while the personal savings rate has averaged only 1.4%.

The point is clear. For the savings rate to return to healthy levels, America must end its reckless creation of debt in the coming years. This means contraction in consumption and de-leveraging. Indeed, excess demand has been eliminated by wealth destruction in the subprime crisis. De-leveraging in the post-bubble period will constrain future demand recovery. This will clearly hurt Asian export growth.

If Asian domestic demand were stronger, that would help lessen the blow from this external shock. But, despite evidence from the 1997/98 Asian crisis showing that too much reliance on external demand as the key growth driver was dangerous, Asia has not learned. The region is still export-dependent, with domestic consumption as a share of GDP falling steadily on the back of a persistent rise in the export share after the Asia crisis (Chart 9.1). Even in China, consumption accounts for only 36% of GDP, compared with almost 70% in the USA. While Chinese investment accounts for 42% of GDP, much of that is export-driven.

De-leveraging will also reduce global capital flows to Asia in all forms – foreign direct investment, portfolio investment and credit. Those economies that have high fiscal deficit and foreign debt (such

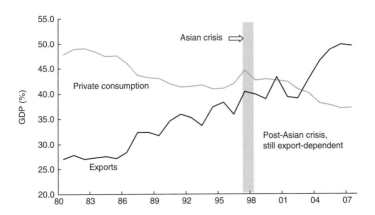

Chart 9.1   Asia has not learned its lessons
Source: CEIC.

as Indonesia, the Philippines and Vietnam; see Chart 9.7) and/or rely heavily on foreign capital inflows to fuel growth (such as India and South Korea) will suffer more in the post-bubble adjustment of the developed world. Asia's current account surpluses will shrink, with many turning into deficits, as already seen in Indonesia, Malaysia, South Korea and Thailand. This means a reduction in liquidity inflow to the region in the coming years, increasing Asia's external financing needs (the sum of current account balance, net foreign direct investment (FDI) flows and net annual debt repayment) and putting a drag on regional growth.

The adverse impact of a reduction in foreign liquidity inflow on growth is best illustrated by India's situation and its growth outlook, as it is one of the Asian countries most affected by the global credit crunch. In recent years, India's GDP has grown at rates much faster than its potential growth rate, due mainly to large capital inflows. Between 2006 and 2008, India's growth rate averaged 9.3%, up from an average of over 6% in the preceding eight years (Chart 9.2). Boosting this accelerating growth trend was a sharp rise in capital inflows, with a lot of that coming in under the disguise of FDI. For example, between 2001 and 2003, India received an average of US$10 billion of capital inflows each year. But the amount of inflows surged to US$107 billion in 2008. Out of this, about US$45

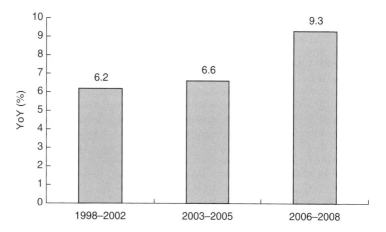

Chart 9.2 Rising Indian GDP growth...
Source: CEIC.

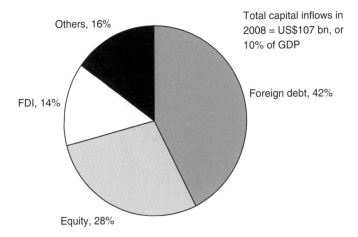

Chart 9.3 ...boosted by capital inflows
Source: CEIC.

billion was foreign borrowing, US$30 billion was equity market-related inflows and only about 15% billion was net FDI (Chart 9.3).

Higher capital inflows had created a seemingly virtuous cycle of an appreciating exchange rate, lower interest rates and strong domestic demand growth, especially in the three years leading up to the US subprime crisis. Indeed, India has one of the strongest credit cycles within Asia, with credit growth rising steadily, higher than nominal GDP growth by a big margin (Chart 9.4). For example, credit growth outpaced nominal GDP growth by 3.8 percentage points in 2006, but that gap grew to 8.6 percentage points in 2008. Unfortunately, capital inflows to India have not been driven by the country's economic fundamentals. This is because India has been running a large current account deficit and fiscal deficit (Charts 9.5 and 9.6). Its foreign debt accounts for about 74% of total foreign reserves. Though this is not excessive by Asian standards (Chart 9.7), it does add to the concerns about India's economic fundamentals when combined with its external and fiscal deficits.

As in many other emerging economies, robust capital inflows to India were dependent on global risk appetite, which, in turn, was driven by the liquidity and growth environment in the developed world before the subprime crisis. Indeed, a large part of the non-debt

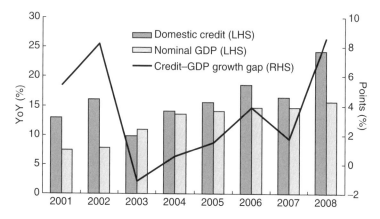

Chart 9.4   Credit growth outpacing GDP growth
Source: CEIC.

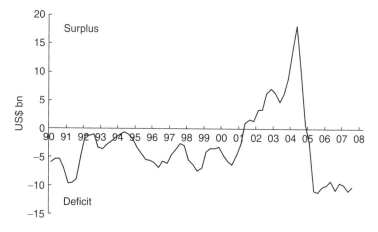

Chart 9.5   India's current account balance
Source: CEIC.

capital inflows to India was estimated to have been funded by way of debt leveraging in the international market. Now that the credit bubble in the western world has burst, sharply cutting risk appetite and capital inflows to emerging markets, India is facing a huge negative growth shock in the coming years due to the dearth of capital inflows. Some analysts estimated that capital inflows to India would

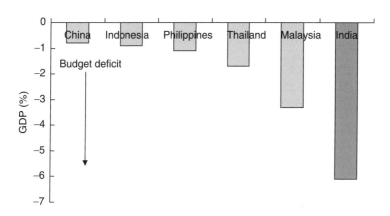

Chart 9.6   India has the worst fiscal balance (2007)
Source: CEIC.

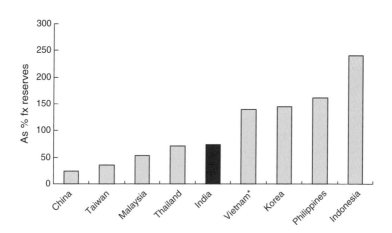

Chart 9.7   Asian foreign debt (1Q08)
Note: * 2007 data.
Source: CEIC.

amount to less than a third of the US$107 billion seen in 2008 for the next three years, if not longer.

Reduced capital inflow to Asia is in fact a form of protectionism in disguise. In the developed world, so much taxpayers' money has been spent on bailing out banks that many of them, including the major global players, will be forced to focus back on their domestic market to give taxpayers their money's worth. In other words, banks that receive state aid are under a lot of political pressure to expand their domestic loan books. This means contraction of foreign lending and, hence, capital outflows towards emerging markets.

Global banks complying with their political masters' command to focus on domestic lending is equivalent to protectionism against the globalisation and free flow of capital. This 'capital protectionism' distorts the allocation of investment on a global scale and hurts trade financing and, consequently, trade in all kinds of goods and services. So it is arguably the worst form of protectionism. In contrast to trade protectionism, which hurts specific goods, capital protectionism destroys every ingredient of globalisation in one stroke. This, in turn, damages productivity of all economies by limiting market forces and scope, resulting in lower economic growth for the whole world.

The post-bubble adjustment

Recessions brought about by the bursting of a nationwide asset bubble are fundamentally different from normal recessions. The bursting of an asset bubble means destruction of private sector balance sheets, as the value of assets bought with borrowed funds implodes while the debt incurred to buy those assets remains at its original value. Many businesses and households may fall into negative net-worth situations. When these private sector agents start paying off debt or increasing savings to regain their financial health and credit ratings, the economy enters a so-called 'balance-sheet recession' (Koo, 2003). In this situation, monetary easing by the central bank will fail to stimulate the economy or the asset market. Interest rate cuts lose their effectiveness because the private sector with a huge debt overhang is not interested in borrowing at any interest rate.

The post-subprime crisis adjustment has started in the large overconsuming economies in the developed world, led by the USA. This first stage of adjustment has eliminated the debt-fuelled consumption binge that enabled their large trade deficits. The second stage of the adjustment involves Asia, whose export growth has been contracting since November 2008. The global balance of payments must balance. So a reduction of consumption by one sector (the developed

world) in the global balance must come with a corresponding adjustment in the other sector (Asia).

There are three ways the global system can adjust. One is for the
underlying global imbalances to remain. Governments of the USA
and other trade-deficit countries can borrow massively to support
aggressive fiscal spending to offset the contraction of household consumption. But, as debt-financed consumption by the likes of the USA
has been one of the root problems for this global 'financial tsunami',
simply replacing one over-consuming American entity by another
cannot be a long-term solution.

The second way is for the trade-surplus countries to sharply raise
domestic consumption, most likely via massive fiscal spending, to
match the decline in the developed world's household consumption.
But this is an impractical way out because the adjustment scale is
way beyond the capacity of most countries to handle. For example, a
fall in US consumption equivalent to 5% of its GDP (which is a low
estimate, given the scale of the economic damages inflicted by the
subprime crisis) would require a rise in Chinese consumption equal
to 17% of China's GDP. This is equivalent to requiring Chinese consumption to grow by 40% a year, a clear impossibility.

This leaves the final way out – a sharp fall in global output, with
massive factory closures, bankruptcies and unemployment, to eliminate overcapacity. The painful burden of this adjustment will fall
on the trade-surplus economies, notably Asia, because this is where
the bulk of the overcapacity is found. As a notable example, most of
China's robust economic growth in the past fifteen years had been
driven by supply-side expansion, supported by strong export growth.
And that robust export growth was sustained by excess consumption
in the western world. As a result, Chinese exports had become the
key driver for domestic investment growth and absorbing the bulk
of the manufacturing excess capacity (Charts 9.8 and 9.9). The economic pain that will result from the needed adjustment will be high
and potentially destabilising.

However, before this adjustment can run its course, which will last
for years, there is a risk that individual Asian countries will try to
avoid the demand contraction and its resulting economic pain by
boosting their ability to export overcapacity through trade-related
measures. This may include export subsidies, subsidised financing,
competitive currency devaluation, import tariffs and the like. The

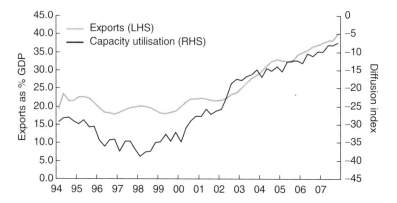

Chart 9.8   Exports absorbing China's capacity utilisation
Source: CEIC.

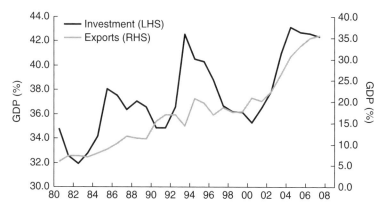

Chart 9.9   Exports driving Chinese investment
Source: CEIC.

incentive for the Asian authorities to do this is strong because there is insufficient domestic growth momentum (see Chart 9.1).

This was in fact the US strategy when, in a similar situation to China today, it was forced to adjust to the 1929/31 crisis. The US had a serious overcapacity problem in 1929. For much of the 1920s, it was able to export its overcapacity by running huge trade surpluses with the rest of the world. But, when the 1929/31 global crisis hit and eliminated the ability of the trade-deficit countries to import, the USA faced an ugly adjustment of output contraction. But it tried to avoid the painful adjustment process by enacting trade tariffs, most notably by the Smoot–Hawley bill of 1930. By doing so, it forced an output contraction on the rest of the world. But the trade-deficit countries fought back with retaliation measures against the USA. Trade wars ensued, resulting in a collapse in international trade. This, in turn, forced the adjustment back to the USA via sharp output contraction, or the Great Depression, as the process was subsequently called.

US overconsumption was one of the root causes of the global imbalance that led to the 'financial tsunami'. In the post-bubble adjustment, consumption by the USA and other spendthrift economies is contracting and the process is pushing up their savings rates. But this is only half of the adjustment needed. The other half must come from the other side of the global imbalance – Asia's overproduction. Asian consumption must rise sharply or a sharp drop in production must ensue. At the time of writing, a few Asian economies, including Hong Kong, Singapore, Korea and Japan, have reported deep economic recession with negative growth rates of over 2% for at least two quarters in a row. More ugly data lie ahead. And, this time around, it is unlikely that the Asian region will be able to stage a V-shaped economic growth rebound as it did after the 1997/98 Asian crisis. This is because the crisis this time is global, with synchronised demand contraction throughout the world, whereas last time the developed world was still growing strongly and absorbing Asian exports to help pull the region out of the Asian crisis.

The post-bubble world

So the coming years of post-bubble adjustment will feature asset price deflation, goods price disinflation, de-leveraging by households in the developed world, overall contraction of the private sector and sub-par economic growth. With nobody borrowing and everybody paying off debt or raising savings, even at zero interest rates, the deflationary spiral becomes a real threat in this situation. This is because those unborrowed savings and debt repayment are leakages from the income stream. If left unattended, the economy will continue to lose aggregate demand equivalent to the unborrowed amount until either private sector balance sheets are repaired or the sector has become too poor to save any money.

On the back of massive private sector retrenchment, the key policy response should be a rise in government spending to keep GDP from falling into a downward spiral. This will create income for households and banks to repair their balance sheets. Monetary easing, even in its extreme form of quantitative easing, is helpful but not sufficient. This is because, when the private sector is de-leveraging, it is in no position to respond to even zero interest rates and ample liquidity.

In the process of balance-sheet repairing, public confidence is weak and the risk of the economy falling into a deflationary spiral is high. Raising government spending is far more effective than a tax cut in boosting domestic demand in this situation because any tax cut will likely be saved or used to pay off debt. Lax monetary policy augmented by big fiscal expansion will also go a long way to remove deflationary expectations, which could easily become self-fulfilling and result in a vicious debt-deflation cycle. History shows that governments have indeed reacted strongly to financial crises by fiscal activism funded by public borrowing. Researchers at the University of Maryland and Harvard University studied thirteen major financial crises in the past and found that, on average, real public debt in the affected countries soared by 86% within three years after the crises occurred. In some cases the increase was over 150% (Reinhart and Rogoff, 2009).

For this subprime crisis, the IMF forecasts that in by 2012 the ratio of gross public debt to GDP could reach 117% in Italy, 97% in the USA, 80% in France and Germany, 75% in the UK and 224% in Japan (IMF, 2009). Though these debt levels may not be too onerous, the IMF concludes, they do point to the expectation that the public sector will grow significantly in the post-crisis years to make up for the losses in private sector output and investment if the authorities want to prevent an economic and financial implosion.

The government should remain active and economic policies should remain expansionary until the credit market is normalised and the private sector balance sheet is repaired. As and when that point is reached, the government must be sensitive enough to withdraw the monetary and fiscal stimuli that it had injected into the system so as to avoid igniting inflation and crowding out private sector investment. As of early 2009, eighteen months after the subprime crisis broke, we are nowhere near that point of policy reversal. Overall, in the coming years, private sector investment and consumption spending will be very weak. Public sector spending will rise sharply to fight the massive deflationary forces of private sector de-leveraging. In both the developed and the developing worlds, infrastructure spending will be the key tool for fiscal activism. It is clear that countries like China and India will need to continue building new roads, ports, railways, industrial parks and power grids, and improving the logistic network. In the developed world, infrastructure spending will mostly take the form of upgrading communication, transport and power links.

In the short term, the post-bubble adjustment will constrain demand growth and keep inflation and interest rates from rising higher. The world will be focused on fighting the deflationary risk. So investments with steady and high yield will be the preferred choice in this environment. Global investment grade corporate bonds are attractive in this context because their yield spreads have soared so high that they are pricing in default rates in a Great Depression situation, which is an unlikely outcome in my view.

In the medium term, there will be an infrastructure boom. Industrial commodities and construction materials will benefit directly. The current commodity bear market will likely turn around by 2010, when most governments – from Asia and China to the G7 countries – begin to ramp up infrastructure spending. In the next two decades, commodity price are likely to remain on a secular bull-market trend. There will be cycles within this secular trend. But each time the commodity market's cyclical downturn will likely hit a bottom higher than the previous one, forming a so-called ascending-bottom trend.

A scared China

There is a worry about China, scared by the devastating impact of the subprime crisis and the failure of the US banking model, shifting its asset holdings in the foreign exchange reserves away from the US dollar significantly in the post-crisis period. Such a move will cause a sell-off in the US dollar, create chaos in the global markets and hurt the global economic recovery in the post-crisis years. China alone accounts for over 27% of the world's total foreign exchange (FX) reserves. If it moved out of the US dollar in search for an alternative reserve currency, other central banks and investors might follow, prompting a crash in the US dollar exchange rate. This alone would force the US Fed to raise interest rates to stem the capital flight, wreaking havoc in the economy and financial system of the USA and, eventually, the world.

Such a shift away from the US dollar would also have huge implications for financial markets beyond exchange rates. Foreign investors, including central banks, are estimated to have held 50% (or US$3.2 trillion) of the US Treasury bond market. China is the largest foreign sovereign holder, accounting for 24% of all foreign holdings. The US Treasury market would crash if China and other sovereign holders started to desert it. That would force a sharp rise in US interest rates, strangling America's corporate bond and mortgage markets. All this would crush the US economy and asset market, sending negative shock waves around the world. This risk may be real, but it is unlikely that China will pursue this action even in the medium term.

The worry about China deserting the US dollar was underscored by the People's Bank of China (China's central bank) governor Zhou Xiaochuan's suggestion on 24 March 2009 of replacing the US dollar by the IMF's Special Drawing Rights (SDR), which are units of a currency basket including the US dollar, euro, sterling and yen, as the world reserve currency. This is a solid idea, which, in essence, implies that China would want to shift out of the US dollar into the SDR. But it is not practical to do so in the short term.

Technically, it would be very complicated to implement the idea of a super-sovereign reserve currency (whether it is in SDR or some other currencies or a currency basket) because of the inertia in the US dollar's global status. Most international trade and financial flows and, hence, the international unit of accounts are based on the US dollar. The global payments and settlement systems are thus dominated by the US dollar also.

It will take a very long time for alternative forms to evolve which can replace the US dollar's international reserve currency and medium of exchange status. Hence, most countries, including China, have very few alternatives but to invest their foreign reserves in US dollar-denominated assets. Crucially, the US fixed income market is the biggest and the most liquid in the world.

Fundamentally, the SDR is not a medium of exchange in the real world. There are no SDR assets at all. The SDR is only a unit of account in the IMF. When the IMF allocates SDRs, the recipient countries exchange them for local currencies at the local central banks. That money is then used to buy goods and services, invest and trade with other countries. No one is using, or will likely use, SDR in international trade.

A more practical question is: who will decide the issuance and the pricing of the SDR – the IMF? Asia and many other emerging economies will almost certainly object to that, given the track record of the IMF's economic prescriptions sending their economies into tailspins. China, in fact, does not want to empower the IMF. That is why, in the G20 summit on 20 April 2009 in London, where Russia proposed an IMF or G20 Working Group to assess the idea of a new global reserve currency, there was no word from China at all, despite its vocal suggestion before the summit.

The point is that that there will be no credible successor to the US dollar for many years to come. No other economies and financial markets are large or deep enough to replace the USA. The euro, or even the Chinese renminbi (RMB), might become an alternative reserve currency down the road, but that is a very long way away. There is also concern that the euro may eventually break up. Meanwhile, using the SDR in actual transaction is very much a longterm idea. Some baby steps are needed first to make it a real currency before one can even think about its role as a reserve currency.

There is also a thought about China replacing some of its US dollar foreign assets by IMF bonds. Throughout its sixty-year history, the IMF had never issued any bonds. At the time of writing, the IMF has not confirmed whether it will issue any bonds to bolster its funding resources for fighting the global 'financial tsunami'. If the IMF does go ahead, its new bonds will provide an alternative low-risk (triple-A rated) asset for China to invest its foreign exchange reserves. But whether China can diversify away from the US dollar depends on whether the IMF bond would be issued in non-US dollar currency, the size of the issue and how much China can buy. It has been suggested that the IMF might issue its debt in SDR terms. No matter what currencies the IMF bonds might be issued in, the foreign exchange diversification effect for China will be small, as 70% of China's foreign exchange reserves are estimated to be in US dollars (20% in euros and the rest mostly in JPY).

If the IMF were to turn to the global bond market to raise funds, it would add to the global debt supply at a time when the global authorities are also issuing record amounts of debt to finance fiscal bailout of the global financial system. This would push up borrowing costs and hurt the global system further. To minimise the impact on borrowing costs, the IMF may not want to issue bonds; it may instead borrow directly from governments via private placements or bilateral loans. Indeed, China agreed in the April 2009 G20 summit to contribute US$40 billion to the IMF, along with Japan and Europe, in the form of a bilateral loan, instead of having the IMF issuing bonds for sale.

So, while IMF bonds are an investment alternative for China's FX reserves, they would not help China to diversify its foreign exchange reserves in any meaningful way. The only achievement for China will be to have a little more say in the IMF via a bigger quota due to its bigger funding contribution to the Fund.

Finally, some analysts also argue that China would massively increase its gold holdings and replace them with its US dollar assets. Currently, China's central bank has about 1% of its total official reserves held in gold, compared with the world's major central bank average of 10% (Chart 9.10). The USA, Germany, France, Italy, Switzerland, the Netherlands and the ECB are the largest gold holders. The USA has almost 79% of its official reserves held in gold, amounting to 8,134 tons (or 27% of world total official gold holdings) as of March 2009.

China's State Administration of Foreign Exchange (SAFE) announced in late April 2009 that the country had increased its gold holdings by 76% to 1,054 tonnes in 2008 from 600 tonnes in 2003. That revelation sparked a rally in gold prices. But, even with that increase over a five-year period, China's gold holdings are still a very small part of its total official asset holdings. So there is great potential for it to increase gold holdings.

However, if China were to increase its gold holdings substantially in a short period of time, it could push up world gold prices sharply, creating a gold bubble. This is because world gold supply is pretty much fixed at around 3,500 tonnes a year. Meanwhile, gold sales by the

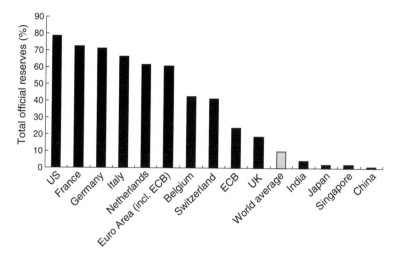

Chart 9.10 World official gold holdings (March 2009)
Source: CEIC.

other central banks are expected to remain small due to the Central Bank Gold Agreement (CBGA), which limits their annual gold sales. On the other hand, China's potential gold-buying power is huge. If China were to use 10% of its US$2 trillion foreign exchange reserves to buy gold, assuming an average gold price of US$850/oz, China could buy 6,671 tonnes of gold with US$200 billion. That would equal 1.92 years of gold supply in one go. Such a surge in demand would certainly disrupt the gold market by pushing the price of gold through the roof. So, practically, China will not do it in a hurry.

But isn't China's revelation of a rise in its gold holdings a sign of more buying to come? Unlikely, in my view. It would make more sense for China to announce a rise in its gold holdings when its buying programme was completed, rather than part-way through it, to avoid chasing rising prices effected by its own purchase announcement.

In a nutshell, if Beijing were to diversify its foreign exchange reserves away from the US dollar into other currencies and/or asset classes in a short time, that would cause a US dollar crisis, create chaos in the global markets and hurt the global economic recovery and, eventually, China's own economy. The move would also hurt the US Treasury market and, hence, the value of China's foreign exchange reserves. It would also disrupt the gold market balance by creating a gold price bubble. Due to these significant disruptive impacts on the world markets and the inertia in the US dollar as the global reserve currency, China is unlikely to move away from the US dollar assets any time soon, despite its intention to do so in order to seek risk diversification benefits. China's FX diversification out of the US dollar is a long-term slow process. It will not be a major event upsetting the post-bubble economy; and it will not be a major investment theme in the medium term, as some analysts would like to believe.

10
China After Subprime

China has been pursuing a development model that is based on supply side expansion, with high savings boosting investment at the expense of consumption. Hence, it has never developed a significant service industry or a financial system capable of channelling savings to consumption via a consumer finance framework. Domestic consumption deficiency has, in turn, pushed the bulk of the industrial capacity towards exports. Since the mid-1990s, when China's exports became a critical mass in global trade, its economic growth has become dependent on the infinite capacity for debt-financed consumption by US households.

However, the subprime crisis has disrupted this growth model, as Americans have to save again in the post-crisis world to rebuild their shattered balance sheets. In this de-leveraging process, the US trade deficit will contract from the pre-crisis record level of over 6% of GDP to levels more consistent with the historical average of 1–2% of GDP. This will, in turn, force an expenditure-switching on the part of China from exports to domestic consumption. Beijing is also trying to push that switch towards domestic spending via fiscal and administrative measures. In November 2008, Beijing announced a huge RMB4 trillion (US$586 billion) fiscal stimulus package for 2009 and 2010 (equivalent to 7% of GDP each year) to combat the negative impact of the 'financial tsunami'. The impact of the fiscal stimulus started to show in early 2009, with major leading economic indicators, such as banking lending, money supply growth, and purchasing managers index, all rebounding from their low points in late 2008. Beijing's powerful fiscal push will make

China the brightest growth spot in the post-subprime world, with growth rate expected to average 7% a year while the western world will be struggling to keep growth rates above zero during the post-bubble adjustment years.

China's battle against the 'financial tsunami' is creating two trends: a stronger consumer sector in China and a more dominant role of the public sector in the economy. While a stronger consumer sector holds the promise of changing China's dependence on exports for growth, history has shown that such a switch is difficult and slow. Meanwhile, increasing government intervention in the economy has the potential of evolving into a roadblock for future growth. (For further analysis on China's ability to sustain long-term growth and its policy vision for the country's economic future, please see Lo 2007.)

The subprime crisis and the Chinese consumer

The subprime crisis has incidentally created a stronger China relative to the developed world, since the Middle Kingdom has not been much affected by the 'credit quake'. In 2008, China replaced Germany as the world's third largest economy in nominal dollar terms. It is approaching the size of the US economy fast and is well on its way to becoming the world's largest auto market, thanks to the collapse in sales in the USA. Recently, capital-rich Chinese firms have also been on a global shopping spree, buying distressed assets and commodities for strategy development. Meanwhile, the country's massive (US$2 trillion at the time of writing) foreign reserves have been regarded as a crucial balancing factor for global interest rates and the foreign exchange market. On a global scale, the rising importance of China, together with other emerging countries, will shape the global economic and geopolitical landscape for the years to come.

However, despite China's rising international influence, it suffers from chronic domestic consumption weakness. This is in sharp contrast to the overextended consumption situation in America and Europe. Chinese household consumption has been falling steadily over the years (Chart 10.1), from an average of over 50% of GDP in the 1980s to about 40% in the 1990s and to only 36% now. Meanwhile, household saving deposits have jumped to almost 70% of GDP from

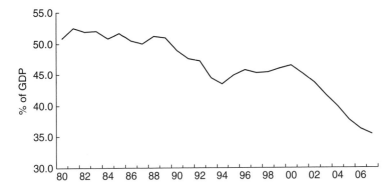

Chart 10.1 Chinese consumption falling steadily
Source: CEIC.

less than 50% two decades ago. Manufacturers are being forced to depend on overseas markets for growth, thus increasing the exposure of the domestic economy to the global business cycle.

On a positive note, the subprime crisis has provided a good opportunity for China to change its growth model. Chinese consumers could well emerge as the key growth engine when the export engine is dying under the weight of the post-crisis multi-year economic adjustment. First, the key reason for Chinese consumers' high propensity to save has been the country's broken safety net. Previously, China's state-owned enterprises (SOEs) provided the country's socialist safety net, including free lodging, transport, medical services, and even food. But those freebies disappeared when the SOE sector collapsed in the late 1990s under Beijing's enterprise reform, which weeded out inefficient SOEs. Government social welfare spending has been rising in recent years but remains insufficient to give its people a sense of security.

For example, Chinese government spending on healthcare was only 1.8% of GDP in 2004 (UNDP 2007–2008; the most recent data available at the time of writing). This compares poorly with 8.1% in Norway, 6.9% in the USA, 6.5% in the Czech Republic, and 3% in Mexico. Meanwhile, Chinese household expenditure on healthcare has increased sharply since the mid-1990s (Chart 10.2). This has, in turn, reduced discretionary buying power for other goods. Crucially, the lack of a sufficient social safety net has adversely

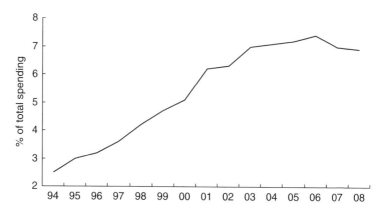

Chart 10.2   Household medical and medicine expenses
Source: CEIC.

affected consumer behaviour by raising precautionary demand for money and, hence, household savings.

In 2008, the central leadership reached a consensus decision to put social coverage expansion at the top of the policy agenda to address the consumption deficiency problem. A series of measures have been adopted, the most concrete being the healthcare reform plan that was started in early 2009. Under this plan, Beijing will spend RMB850 billion (US$125 billion), or 3% of GDP, between 2009 and 2011 to provide medical insurance for at least 90% of the population. Beijing is also trying to boost rural consumption by raising rural income. If successful, this will yield some effective results, because the marginal propensity to consume of the poor rural population is much higher than that of the rich urban population.

To boost rural income, the government has been cutting agricultural taxes and fees, increasing fiscal transfers to the farmers, raising minimum procurement prices for agricultural goods, and starting to provide some basic medical and pension coverage for the rural population. Further, to fight the negative economic impact of the subprime crisis, the government has started in 2009 to provide rural households with direct subsidies for buying white goods, such as home appliances and electronics. All this is meant to release pent-up demand in the countryside, where currently possession of consumer electronics and electrical appliances and consumer

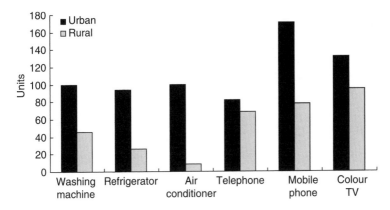

Chart 10.3   Consumer goods/100 households
Source: CEIC.

durable goods accounts for less than half of that of urban house-holds (Chart 10.3).

Over the longer term, Chinese consumers will also benefit from further financial liberalisation, with the government aiming at developing the consumer finance market. At the moment, house-hold debt in China accounts for only 12% of GDP, compared with over 100% in some developed countries, such as Australia, the USA and the UK. Furthermore, over 85% of China's household debt is in mortgages. This implies that leveraged consumption, such as credit cards, car loans and instalment credit, is extremely limited. To help better manage credit risk and build an infrastructure for consumer lending, the government has developed a nationwide personal credit monitoring system. With massive liquidity on their balance sheets, as seen in their low (65%) average loan-to-deposit ratio, Chinese banks are in a much stronger position than ever before to increase lending to consumers.

It is unrealistic, however, to expect a massive consumption boom in China in the near future because it will take a long time for the above trends to fully develop. But there is no doubt that domes-tic consumption has been deeply depressed by the skewed supply-side expansion growth model. With massive household savings, an under-leveraged consumer sector and improving social welfare, it is very likely that the average Chinese consumption power will grow significantly in the coming years. A stronger consumer sector will reduce China's dependence on external demand as a source of growth and enhance the country's growth sustainability. This is especially crucial in the coming years because consumers in the developed world will be stuck in a structural downward adjustment trend.

Loser-picking strategy

Beijing has not just focused on the consumer sector. It has been engineering an overall strategic policy shift from boosting growth quantity to improving growth quality in recent years. Arguably, its controlled and selective macro tightening measures between 2005 and 2008 were part of the expenditure-switching initiatives. For example, administrative measures were imposed to curb export growth and investment in base metals and other energy and resource-intensive high-pollution industries. In its development strategy, Beijing has never wanted to cut growth across the board. Instead, it has tried to pick 'losers' (those sectors and industries that are deemed excessive and redundant) and eliminate them by selective administrative means.

This 'loser-picking' exercise is exactly opposite to the 'winner-picking' policy that the Asian economies used in the 1960s and 1970s for economic development. Back then, industrialisation began with the Asian governments cherry-picking industries and sectors which they favoured. But China's growth has been driven by supply-side expansion from industries of all sorts since the 1990s, creating massive excess capacity across the board, from beer to cars, white goods to metals, to name just a few. Thus, Beijing is now trying to clean up its economic development strategy by shifting away from quantity growth to quality growth to sustain the country's long-term growth potential.

Some initial signs are showing that this expenditure-switching strategy might be starting to shift China's growth structure towards the right direction – less growth in exports and investment but more in consumption (Chart 10.4). To boost consumption, the authorities have been implementing policies to facilitate urbanisation, to improve the social safety net, labour mobility and protection, and to shift income distribution towards the rural poor, though there is still a long way to go for these measures to reach their end goals. Meanwhile, measures have been put in place to cut export and investment growth.

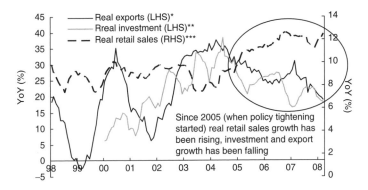

Chart 10.4 Initial signs of structural shift in growth

Notes: All series are 6mma.
* deflated by HK re-export prices.
** deflated by corporate good prices.
*** deflated by CPI.

Source: CEIC.

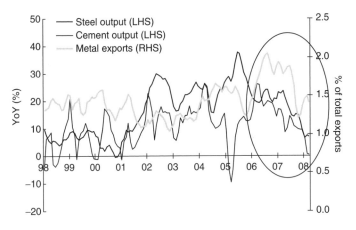

Chart 10.5 Growth rebalancing*

Note: * All series in 3-mth moving averages.

Source: CEIC.

The government's efforts to downsize and discourage the export of industries with excess capacity and potential for significant environmental damage have also shown some initial results. For example, output growth of steel and cement has plunged from over 20% a year

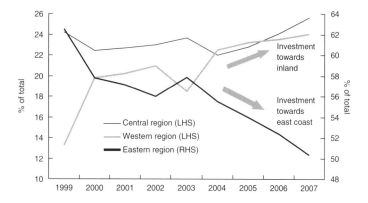

Chart 10.6   Investment reshuffling towards inland
Source: CEIC.

to below 10% since 2006, while the export share of metals has fallen by over half (Chart 10.5). Finally, investment growth has been shifting from the rich eastern seaboard to the central and western regions (Chart 10.6), reflecting the initial success of the government's investment reshuffling strategy to boost the regional laggards.

The consumption blues

These initial structural shifts may seem encouraging, but history has shown that the transitions will not be easy. Like the USA and Japan during their export-reliant growth phases, China has not yet done enough to make that structural shift entrenched. These initial trends could be reversed if Beijing loses structural reform momentum. This risk is especially prominent in the post-subprime adjustment years because the global contraction stemming from the external shock could easily soften the Chinese authorities' resolve to sustain short-term economic pains for long-term gains. In other words, the post-crisis economic difficulties could make it difficult for China to move away from exports to consumption, despite some genuine intention to do so.

This can clearly be seen in the stubborn 'export-led' mindset entrenched in some government officials. For example, Chinese Commerce Minister Chen Deming announced on 9 March 2009, while the annual National People's Congress was being held in Beijing, that China would reduce export taxes to zero and give more financial support to exporters in order to gain market share of global trade in the subprime crisis environment. 'We should increase our share of the global market. ... We must transform ourselves from a big export nation to a strong export nation', the *Financial Times* reported (*Financial Times*, 2009).

If China had been sufficiently pushing the structural shift to greater domestic consumption, its export industries would have shrunk before the 'financial tsunami', more robust finance and service sectors catering to local consumers would have been developed, and capital and labour would have been reallocated throughout the economy. But, because of the insufficient effort made in the pre-crisis years, even now that Beijing wants to speed up the shift in the post-crisis years, it just cannot do so effectively. Despite billions of dollars of fiscal pump-priming, China's trade surplus still widened from an already-high US$17 billion monthly average in the first half of 2008 to US$33 billion in the second half of the year. In January 2009, the monthly trade surplus even soared to US$39 billion. Granted, the surplus will likely narrow as the subprime shock deepens further, but the point is clear – China's pump-priming to boost domestic growth has not been working effectively. Otherwise, the trade surplus should have come down persistently during the subprime crisis, with rising imports on the back of falling exports.

The stimulus had not worked as effectively as expected to boost consumption because the money had not gone into where it was supposed to go – the consumers and the service industries. The service industry was almost non-existent, and it was extremely hard to boost consumption when people's confidence was weak (a result of the combination of the global crisis impact and an insufficient domestic social safety network). So Beijing's effort to boost domestic demand had found its way mostly into investment (infrastructure projects) and the manufacturing sector, especially to the large SOEs. For example, 70% of the RMB4 trillion stimulus package that Beijing announced in November 2008 went into infrastructure investment and post-earthquake construction. Only 1% was designated for medical spending and 7% for providing affordable housing. Other elements of the fiscal stimulus programmes included promoting company restructuring and offering subsidised loans to support technical innovations within the non-ferrous metals sector; giving tax rebates for electronics and information technology product exports; and increasing tax rebates for textile producers.

Thus, the stimulating effects of these measures had mostly shown up in boosting output rather than consumption directly. The result was to keep employment and boost consumption. But this was done indirectly, by boosting manufacturing capacity (and hence consumption of the workers hired in the factories), rather than by boosting consumption demand directly. As a result, although exports were falling, Chinese output capacity was falling at a slower pace than Chinese consumption. Since a trade surplus is by definition the excess of a country's output over its consumption, China's trade surplus will not fall meaningfully if Beijing keeps boosting domestic demand by increasing investment and manufacturing capacity. This will only make it more difficult for China to shake off its reliance on external demand.

China will eventually make that shift from export-led growth to domestic-driven growth, but no one should expect it to be fast and easy. As much as Beijing would like to change its growth model, it cannot do so quickly except by tolerating a massive collapse in manufacturing output. For the sake of stability, China does not want to do that. The world will also suffer from a China shock if its manufacturing sector collapses suddenly. So, in the post-subprime world, both China and the global economy are stuck between a rock and a hard place – while it is clear that China must make that expenditure-switching to its growth model as soon as possible, it will not be possible to do so quickly. China's growth transition from one development model to another is a long-drawn-out process. Political tension, often manifested in trade and capital protectionism, between China and the crisis-hit western world will mount under these circumstances.

More government intervention

Unlike in the USA and some other developed countries, where the prospects of partial nationalism of the banking system and fiscal activism have raised fears among investors of bigger governments, state support in China is not a taboo. The growth boost campaign that started in November 2008 in China was swiftly implemented as soon as Beijing decided to do so. It consisted of huge public spending on public projects and state support for major industries. Beijing, in fact, singled out ten major industries for state preferential treatment to prevent their collapse. Rightly or wrongly, these are near-term fiscal measures needed to prevent the economy from falling into a downward spiral. However, there is a risk that they might reflect a tendency of the leadership and policymakers to return to big government again, using the weakening economy as an excuse.

The risk of that tendency is seen in the steady rise in government spending as a share of GDP since the Asian crisis in 1997/98 (Chart 10.7). When economic reform started in 1978, government spending fell persistently until 1998. Continued economic liberalisation had dismantled the inefficient state sector and developed a burgeoning private sector, which, in turn, led to significant efficiency gains in the economy. All this formed a strong foundation for China's economic success in the past thirty years. However, in 1998 the Chinese authorities started using counter-cyclical fiscal policy to sustain growth to fight the economic shock from the Asian crisis. Since then, government spending as a share of GDP has been rising steadily. This ratio is likely to continue to rise in the coming years, as Beijing will continue to use fiscal pump-priming to counteract the aftershock of the global subprime crisis. There will

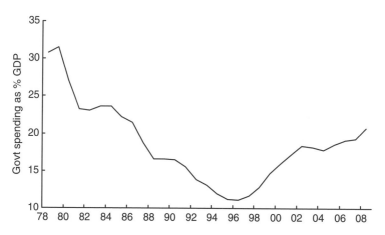

Chart 10.7   Big government is returning
Source: CEIC.

be more mega-infrastructure projects, social welfare spending and fiscal support for various industries. All this means a bigger government down the road.

It is too early to conclude at this time whether a bigger government in the Chinese economy is necessarily bad, especially when all other governments, from the USA, the UK and Europe to the Asian regional governments, are all increasing their role in the economy to fight the 'financial tsunami'. At this point, Chinese government expenditures also do not seem to be excessive, as compared with other countries in terms of public sector debt to GDP ratio (Chart 10.8). In fact, China's public debt is even lower than the average of the emerging market governments. However, compared with China's previous reform trend, which was focused on economic liberalisation and reduced government intervention, the recent development is a noticeable change in policy intention that warrants monitoring.

In the short term, the impact of these changes may not be important. But, beyond the subprime crisis, whether China continues to loosen control on economic activity and move towards further policy liberalisation will have profound implications for the economy's long-term growth outlook and asset values. There is still a lot of rigidity in the Chinese economic system. For example, the capital

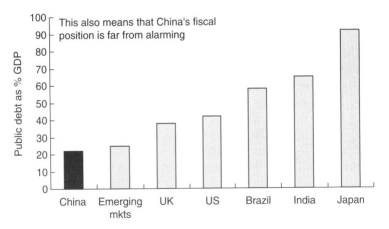

Chart 10.8 Relative size of the public sector*
Note: * data as of 2008.
Source: CEIC.

account is still not convertible, the banking system is still largely government-controlled, the capital markets are still underdeveloped, and the service sector is still heavily regulated. The government still routinely uses administrative measures and other intervention tools, like moral suasion and political pressure, to direct industrial development. All these create distortions and unintended impact on the social and economic fronts. Hence, continued policy liberalisation, rather than more intervention, is the way to sustain growth.

Increasing intervention in the economy will also put the government's credibility to the test. This will, in turn, create downside risk for policy actions and social responses. For example, achieving an 8% GDP growth in the aftermath of the subprime crisis was an explicit target that Beijing stressed repeatedly in 2009 to counteract the external shock. And Beijing appeared to be doing all it could to create jobs and boost consumption. With enormous financial resources at their disposal, the authorities' reflation campaign seemed to be highly credible and the Chinese people had high hopes that the government could deliver its promises. At the time of writing, however, the subprime crisis is far from over. There is still a chance that it may worsen further before stabilising. This means that there is a possibility of grave disappointment among the Chinese if the global economy falls into a prolonged recession that dwarfs Beijing's reflation effort to protect its economy. In this case, the risk of social tension and even unrest will mount, putting the authorities in an ever-challenging situation.

While the risk of social unrest on the back of a bad economy is always there, that risk has, in my view, actually been lowered in China in recent years and despite the stress from the 'financial tsunami'. First, the government has employed a populist approach in recent years, with the top leaders reaching out to the people whenever there is a negative economic shock or natural disaster, such as flooding, earthquake, snowstorm or plant closures due to the 'financial tsunami'. This has earned Beijing a lot of good will and support from the people. Second, the government has worked hard to protect employment by implementing massive infrastructure projects to absorb workers, whether they are skilled or not. Beijing has also restored many tax benefits to the labour-intensive processing trade to help ease the labour market pains. In early 2009, for example, the government began to offer full refunds of tuition fees to encourage university graduates to work in the central and western provinces, where economic growth has been rising in recent years but talent has been lacking. Third, Beijing has also been working aggressively to improve the social safety net for the broader population, both as a means to increase consumption and as a way to ease social discontent. In particular, the government is planning to spend RMB850 billion, or 3% of GDP, on increasing basic medical insurance coverage for 90% of the urban workforce by 2011.

In a nutshell, China's fierce battle against the global subprime crisis will create a stronger consumer sector and a bigger government in the coming years. The former holds the promise of becoming the key growth driver for China, putting its economy onto a more sustainable and less volatile growth path. But this trend will take some years to fully develop. Any expectations that China could turn itself into a domestic-driven economy in the next couple of years, especially when the global adjustment to the subprime crisis will still be ongoing, would be unrealistic. Meanwhile, increasing government intervention in the economy has the potential to evolve into a roadblock for long-term growth.

Bibliography

Aghion, P. and Howitt, P. (1992) 'A Model of growth through Creative Destruction', *Econometrica* 60:2, 323–51.

Bhagwati, J. (2008) 'We Need to Guard Against Destructive Creation', *Project MUSE Journals Callaloo* 31:4, The Johns Hopkins University Press, Fall 2008.

Bloomberg (2009) 'Bernanke Says Insurer AIG Operated Like a Hedge Fund', 3 March 2009.

Calvano, E. (2007) 'Destructive Creation', Working Paper Series in Economics and Finance, no. 653, Toulouse School of Economics and Department of Economics, Harvard University.

Financial Times, 'AIG Still Faces Huge Credit Losses', front page, 4 March 2009.

Financial Times, 'China Acts to Shore Up Weakening Exports', 10 March 2009.

Huang, Y. (2008) *Capitalism with Chinese Characteristics*, Cambridge University Press.

International Monetary Fund, 'The State of Public Finances: Outlook and Medium-term Policies After the 2008 Crisis', the Fiscal Affairs Department, March 2009.

Klingbiel, D. *et al* (2002) 'Managing the Real and Fiscal Costs of Banking Crises', World Bank Discussion Papers 428.

Koo, R. (2003) *Balance Sheet Recession – Japan's Struggle with Uncharted Economics and its Global Implications*, John Wiley & Sons (Asia) Pte Ltd.

Krugman, P. (1998) 'What Happened to Asia?', Unpublished manuscript, Massachusetts Institute of Technology, Cambridge.

Krugman, P. (2009) *The Return of Depression Economics and the Crisis of 2008*, Norton.

Lo, C. (2007) *Understanding China's Growth, Forces that Drive China's Economic Future*, Palgrave Macmillan.

Lo, C. (2003) *When Asia Meets China in the New Millennium – China's role in shaping Asia's post-crisis economic transformation*, Pearson Prentice Hall.

Minsky, H. (1992) 'The Financial Instability Hypothesis', Levy Economics Institute Working Paper 74, New York.

Reinhart, C. and Rogoff, K.S. (2009) 'The Aftermath of Financial Crisis', NBER Working Paper no. 14656, January 2009.

Read, C. (2009) *Global Financial Meltdown: How We Can Avoid The Next Economic Crisis*, Palgrave Macmillan.

Schumpeter, J. (1975) *Capitalism, Socialism and Democracy*, New York: Harper [originally published 1942].

Shiller, R. (2008) *The Subprime Solution: How Today's Global Financial Crisis Happened and What to Do about It?*, Princeton University Press.

Taleb, N.N. (2007) *The Black Swan*, Random House.

Taylor, J. (2009) *Getting off Track: How Government Actions and Interventions Caused, Prolonged and Worsened the Financial Crisis*, Hoover Press.

TWN Third World Network, 'Asia Hit Again – What Lessons Now?', 13 February 2009.

United Nations Development Programme (UNDP), Human Development Report, 2007–2008.

Zandi, M. (2008) *Financial Shock: A 360° Look at the Subprime Mortgage Implosion, and How to Avoid the Next Financial Crisis*, FT Press.

Index

Adjustable rate mortgages (ARM), 10
Administrative measures, 45, 46
AIG
  Collapse, 5, 25, 61, 62–5
  Fed rescue, 63–64
  lesson for China, 61, 64–9
  regulatory loopholes,
    5, 61–3, 64, 65
Asia's response to subprime, 53–8
Asian crisis and subprime crisis,
    1–3, 15–24, 53, 77
  lessons learnt, 11
  lessons not learnt, 18, 93–8
Asset bubbles, 2, 12, 14, 16, 18
Asset deflation, 15, 22
Asset liability mismatch, 61, 64, 65

Bailouts,
  coordination, 52–3
  endogenous vs
    exogenous risks, 20
  objectives, 58
  painful lessons, 58–60
Balance sheet mismatch, 9, 22, 72
Balance sheet recession, 98
Black swan event, 3, 4, 15–18, 22

Capital protectionism, 6, 98, 118
Carry trade, 18
China can't save the world, 41–2, 99
China, lopsided growth, 42–4
China's response to subprime, 54–5
Chinese banks,
  expososure to subprime, 26
  fundamentals, 27–8, 37
  post-crisis risks, 46–8
Collateralised debt obligations
  (CDOs), 2, 3, 8, 9, 10, 62, 64, 72
Coordinated bailouts, 52–3
Counterparty risk, 1, 10, 23, 25, 28
Creative destruction, xiii, 5, 41

Credit bubble and ECB, 13–14
Credit default swaps (CDS), 61, 62,
    63, 66, 73
  dynamic credit pricing, 66
  implications for China, 66–7
  unintended consequences, 67–9
Credit quake, xi, 7, 9, 10, 58, 77, 110
Crisis response, 49–58
Current account deficit/surplus,
    16, 21, 44, 92, 95

Debt-deflation, 25, 35–8, 59, 85, 87,
    101, 102
Decoupling, 39–41
Deflation,
  China's challenge, 89–90
  good vs bad, 35–6
De-leveraging, 15, 22, 36, 37, 53, 69,
    83, 87, 91, 93, 101, 102, 103, 109
Deregulation, 71–3
Destructive creation, xiii, 5, 77–8
Dynamic credit pricing, 66

ECB and credit bubble, 13–14
Europe's response to subprime,
    49–50
Excess capacity, 47, 99, 100, 114, 115
Excess consumption, 42, 92, 101
Excess savings, 42, 43, 92, 111
Expenditure-switching,
    109, 114, 118
Export-led growth model,
    xii, 15, 18, 22, 44, 91–3

Financial contagion, 53, 54, 55, 61
Financial crisis,
  Japan's experience, 59
Financial innovation,
  deregulation, 12, 23, 24, 47, 59,
    61, 71–3
  destructinve creation, xiii, 5, 77–8

Financial tsunami, xi, 7, 9, 10, 11, 15, 38, 99, 101, 105, 109, 110, 117, 120, 121
  securitisation, 7–10
Fortis collapse, 5, 71, 75–6
  lesson for China, 76, 78

Glass-Steagall Act, 71
Global saving-investment imbalance, 4
Global status, US dollar, 104–5, 108
Globalisation, 39, 98
Good bank bad bank model, 59–60

High-power money, 81, 86
Hong Kong's response to subprime, 56

Impact on China, subprime, Chinese banks, 25–9, 46–8
  debt-deflation spiral, 25, 35–8
  macroeconomic policy, 29–31, 44–6
  trade and domestic demand, 31–4
India's response to subprime, 56
Infrastructure boom, 91, 103

Japan's financial crisis, 59
Japan's QE experience, 5–6, 79, 83, 85–7
Japan's response to subprime, 55

Korea's response to subprime, 55–6

Lehman Brothers collapse, 5, 25, 71, 74–5
Lessons for China,
  AIG's collpase, 61, 64–9
  Fortis' collapse, 76, 78
  Lehman Brothers' collapse, 70, 76, 78
Liquidity crisis, 7, 10, 11, 50, 61
Liquidity trap, 82, 88
Loan-to-deposit ratio, 16, 27, 37, 53, 113

Lopsided growth, China, 42–4
Loser-picking strategy, 114–16
L-shape growth, xii

Macro financial innovation failure, 77
Minsky hypothesis, 2
Money multiplier, 81–2, 84, 86
Money velocity, 82, 84
Moral hazard, 1, 2, 12, 16, 20, 58, 61, 66, 67
Mortgage-backed securities (MBS), 2, 3, 8, 9, 10, 62, 63

Negative net-worth, 98
Ninja loans, 2
Non-financial innovation, creative destruction, xiii, 77–8

Originate and distribute model, 3

Pakistan's response to subprime, 57
Ponzi games, 12
Post-subprime world, 101–3
  adjustment process, 98–101
  Asia's defence, 58
  global banking environment, 70, 76
  increase in Chinese government intervention, 6, 110, 118–22
  rise of Chinese consumerism, 6, 110–14
Principle-agent problem, 3
Protectionism, capital vs trade, 6, 97, 98, 118

Quantitative easing, xii, 5, 11, 23, 79–81, 102
  impact on inflation, 79–83
  impact on the US dollar, 79, 83–5
  Japan's failure, 5–6, 79, 83, 85–7
  lessons for China, 88, 89–90
  lessons for the USA, 85, 88

Recapitalisation, 50, 51, 60, 88
Regulatory failure, 12, 46–7, 61, 62, 64–5, 69

Regulatory loopholes, 5, 61–3, 69
  AIG, 64–5
Re-regulation of banks, 22–3
Risk diversification problems, 72
Root cause, subprime crisis,
  59, 60, 77

Saving-consumption imbalance, 92
Savings & Loan crisis, 19
Scandinavian banking crisis, 59, 60
Securitisation, 3, 7–9, 61, 71, 74,
  77, 92
Singapore's response to
  subprime, 56
Social safety net, 43
Solvency crisis, 7, 10, 11, 50, 51, 61
Speical Drawing Rights (SDR),
  104, 105
Structural changes,
  China, 44, 110–14, 118–22
  financial liberalisation, 46–7
Subprime crisis,
  adjustment process, 19–21,
    98–101
  and Asian crisis, 1–3, 15–24
  Asian connection, 18
  Asia's response, 49, 53–8
  black swan event, 3, 4, 15–18, 22
  China's response, 54–5
  Chinese bank risks, 26–8, 47–8
  collateralised debt obligatins
    (CDOs), 2, 3, 8, 9, 10, 62, 64, 72
  conflict of interest problem, 3
  definition, 7–8
  end game, 21–3
  good bank bad bank model,
    59–60

  greed and imprudence, 1–2, 61
  Hong Kong's response, 56
  impact on China, 25–38
  India's response, 56
  Japan's response, 55
  Korea's response, 56
  lessons from bailout, 58–60
  Minsky hypothesis, 2
  mortgage-backed securities,
    2, 3, 8, 9, 10, 62, 63
  Pakistan's response, 57
  regulatory failure, 12, 46–7, 61,
    62, 64–5, 69
  root cause, 59, 60, 77
  Singapore's response, 56
  the seed of the crisis,
    11–14, 59, 60
  the wrong signal, xii, 4, 23–4
  UK's response, 51–2
  unexpected shock, 1
  USA's response, 50–1
  western world's response, 49–53
Supply-side expansion, China, 44–5,
  99, 109, 114

Trade protectionism, 6, 98, 118
Troubled Asset Relief Programme
  (TARP), 50–1, 52

UK's response to subprime, 51–2
Under-consumption, 47
Undervalued RMB, 46–7
Universal banks, 5, 70, 72, 76
US dollar global status, 104–5, 108
USA's response to subprime, 50–1

Zero interest rate policy (ZIRP), 85